When Dinnerbells Ring

Published by:
Talladega, Alabama
Junior Welfare League
P.O. Box 144
Talladega, Alabama 35160
1978

Recipes contributed by members of the Talladega, Alabama Junior Welfare League, their relatives and friends.

"... When dinnerbells ring and we all fly to eat
at the bountiful table of love
Why there's a suggestion that I want to make
To the Master who rules us above,
Give my honey and milk to somebody else
And put down on my plate, if you please,
Cornbread and onions and piled alongside
A big helping of plain blackeyed peas..."
From "A Heavenly Wish"
Woodsmoke II
by Tom Abernethy

First Printing 1978 — 5,000 copies
Second Printing 1979 — 5,000 copies
Third Printing 1981 — 5,000 copies
Fourth Printing 1985 — 5,000 copies
Fifth Printing 1993 — 2,000 copies

International Standard Book Number 0-918544-95-5

Printed in the USA by

When Dinnerbells Ring

Mrs. James W. Heacock, Jr.
Chairman — 1977

Mrs. Jack R. Edmiston
Chairman — 1978

Committee

Mrs. Larry H. Barksdale
Mrs. Michael H. Cleckler
Mrs. Curtis C. Lackey
Mrs. Alden Limbaugh
Mrs. James D. Luker, Jr.
Mrs. William B. McGehee, III
Mrs. Ray Miller
Mrs. Charles Nelson
Mrs. Michael Reeves
Mrs. O. Stanley Thornton
Mrs. Ken H. Wallis

Active Members

Mrs. David B. Beasley
Mrs. Walter Burt
Mrs. Lonnie L. Clevenger
Mrs. T. C. Copeland
Mrs. Toby Deese
Mrs. Wallis Elliott, Jr.
Mrs. Jerry N. Gurley
Mrs. George Hartsfield
Mrs. John D. Hill
Mrs. William C. Hurst, Jr.
Mrs. Guy H. Kaylor
Mrs. William W. Lawrence
Mrs. Tony L. McKinney
Mrs. R. E. Mullins
Mrs. Crawford Nelson
Mrs. Carl R. Reaves
Mrs. Randall Stewart
Mrs. Stephen F. Syer
Mrs. Jimmy E. Woodard

Cover art by Sarah Whitson
Art in Special Menu Section by Wilmary Elliott

Proceeds from the sale of *When Dinnerbells Ring* will be used for community projects sponsored by the Junior Welfare League of Talladega.

When Dinnerbells Ring

Committee — 1993

Mrs. Dyron Overton — Chairman

Mrs. Joe Tom Armbrester
Mrs. Kent Davenport
Mrs. Larry Edmiston
Mrs. Gary Haisten
Mrs. Rick Barber
Mrs. Ricky Lawson
Mrs. Marty Phillips
Mrs. James Pressley
Mrs. Jerry Studdard

Active Members — 1993

Ms. Samantha Armstrong
Mrs. Mike Baker
Ms. Judy Barber
Mrs. Gerald Bittle
Mrs. Robert Blackwell
Mrs. Bill Browning
Mrs. Jeffry Camp
Mrs. Chris Campbell
Mrs. Dennis Dase
Mrs. Steve Freeman
Mrs. Terry Graham
Mrs. Andy Hardy
Mrs. Bill Hopewell
Mrs. Larry Jones
Mrs. John Locklin
Mrs. Stan Mitchell
Mrs. Jake Montgomery
Mrs. Kerry Otwell
Mrs. Mike Patterson
Mrs. Charles Roden
Mrs. Mike Riley
Mrs. Bobby Williams

The Talladega Junior Welfare League

The Talladega Junior Welfare League was organized by 14 dedicated ladies in 1932. It is one of the oldest charity leagues in the state. The charter members gave to the League its purpose: "to foster interest among its members in the social, economic, cultural, and civic conditions of their community, and to make efficient their volunteer services. . ." Each year every league member contributes 60 or more service hours and thousands of dollars to worthy needs of the community.

In addition to $600.00 a year provided for emergency needs of citizens of the community, some of our other contributions are:

Citizens Hospital - The League has provided patients and waiting rooms with current reading material and has operated a hospital cart allowing patients to purchase various items. Recent donations to the hospital have included $5,000.00 toward the purchase of an EKG machine, a "Heart Beat Bear" for the nursery, and support for the car seat program.

Talladega City School System - League members have provided enrichment programs for elementary students. The League has also donated thousands of dollars to the school system for educational materials and computers.

Alabama Institute for Deaf and Blind - The League has purchased play equipment for the preschool program. Members have also hosted a reception for a visually and hearing impaired workshop and have assisted patients at the Orthopedic Clinic in Dowling Infirmary on the AIDB campus.

Meals on Wheels - With the cooperation of Citizens Hospital, hot meals are delivered three days a week to the elderly or disabled.

Heritage Hall Museum - The community is proud of the museum and the League has contributed money toward its renovation. League members have served as docents and have hosted receptions for museum functions.

Red Door Kitchen - In support of a community soup kitchen for the hungry, the League has purchased a freezer and has prepared special dishes to be served.

North Talladega County Association for Retarded Citizens - The League has donated $5,500.00 to the Burton Developmental Center.

The Talladega Junior Welfare League has supported Operation Santa Claus, Birmingham Children's Hospital, Talladega Sunset Inn Retirement Home, Talladega Nursing Home, Talladega Public Library, Leukemia Society, and Salvation Army Shoes for the Needy.

Well known for ante bellum mansions lining oak canopied streets, Talladega, Alabama, is a thriving community nestled in the foothills of the Appalachians; the epitome of gracious southern living and hospitality at its best. The abundance of superb recipes, the pride of many hostesses, was the inspiration for our book. "A Heavenly Wish", a poem from Tom Abernethy's *Woodsmoke II,* was the source of the title. Special thanks go to Mrs. Louise Abernethy for her generosity in allowing us to entitle our book, *When Dinnerbells Ring*. The cookbook committee would also like to express gratitude to Sarah Whitson for time spent on our lovely cover depicting The Pilgrimage Inn, constructed in 1843. Our sincere appreciation also goes to Wilmary Elliott for delighting us with permission to use pen and inks from her book, *East Street South,* in our special menu section. Please use and enjoy this collection of tested recipes with confidence.

THE EDITORS

TABLE OF CONTENTS

Purefoy Hotel
by Alice Jones

Starters

appetizers

MUSHROOM TURNOVERS

"You won't be sorry you went to the trouble to fix these."

1 cup butter
1 8-ounce package cream cheese
½ teaspoon salt
2 cups flour
1 egg yolk
2 teaspoons cream

Mix butter, cream cheese, and salt until smooth. Add flour and continue to mix. Flatten dough into 8 x 6-inch rectangle and chill several hours or overnight. Divide dough in half and roll each into 9 x 6-inch rectangle. Knead once and roll until ⅛ inch thick. Cut into 2½-inch rounds. Place one teaspoon of filling (see below) into center of each round. Moisten edges and fold over; seal with fork. Place on ungreased baking sheet. Combine egg yolk and cream; brush on rounds. Chill one hour or freeze prior to baking. Bake at 350 degrees for 25-30 minutes or until brown. Serve warm or cold. Makes 5-6 dozen.

Filling:

2 4-ounce cans mushrooms, sliced and drained
½ cup onion, minced
2 tablespoons butter
½ teaspoon salt
½ teaspoon pepper
1 teaspoon lemon juice
2 teaspoons flour
½ cup half-half cream
1 tablespoon sherry or vermouth

Sauté mushrooms and onions in butter for 5 minutes. Add next three ingredients and stir. Simmer 2 minutes. Add flour and cream; continue to simmer. Stir in sherry and chill for several hours.

Mrs. William B. McGehee, III (Evelyn)

PARTY CHEESE BALL

2 8-ounce packages cream cheese, softened
2 cups Cheddar cheese
1 tablespoon pimento, chopped
2 tablespoons Worcestershire sauce
3 tablespoons onion, finely chopped
1 teaspoon lemon juice
Dash cayenne pepper
Dash salt
½ cup nuts, chopped

Combine cheeses and mix until blended. Add remaining ingredients except nuts. Shape into ball and roll in nuts. Chill. Garnish with parsley and serve with crackers.
Mrs. Hardy Conner (Becky)

TOMATO DIP

"Delicious with Dorito's or Tortilla chips."

2 fresh tomatoes, skinned
1 10-ounce can Old El Paso tomatoes with green chilies or chili peppers
1 6-ounce can tomato sauce
1 large onion, chopped
1 teaspoon Worcestershire sauce
Dash garlic salt
Dash salt
Dash pepper
Tabasco sauce to taste

In saucepan, boil tomatoes about 5 minutes. Add remaining ingredients and boil 5 minutes. Cool; refrigerate at least 2 hours before serving.
Mrs. Alden Limbaugh (Bobbie)

SHRIMP DIP

1 4½-ounce can shrimp
1 3-ounce package cream cheese
¼ teaspoon onion, grated
¼ teaspoon Worcestershire sauce
1 teaspoon lemon juice
Dash Tabasco sauce
⅓ cup mayonnaise
⅓ cup milk, if needed

Mix all ingredients together; use milk if mixture is stiff. Serve with chips or crackers.
Mrs. Lonnie Clevenger (Mary Burk)

CHEESE EMPINADA

1 package pastry mix
2 cups sharp Cheddar cheese, finely grated
2 4-ounce cans chilies peppers, drained, deseeded, and chopped
½ cup sharp Cheddar cheese, grated
1 10-ounce can taco sauce

Mix pastry by package directions. Add cheese; mix well. Place on floured board and roll ¼ to ⅛ inch thick. Cut into 2½-inch circles. Mix peppers and cheese. Place scant teaspoonful mixture on circle; fold and seal edges tightly. Place on baking sheet; bake at 425 degrees for 10-12 minutes. Serve hot with taco sauce as dip. Can be made ahead and frozen before baking. Serves 8.
Mrs. Tony McKinney (Jeanne)

PIZZA BITES

2 10-count cans Hungry Jack flaky biscuits
1½ pounds beef, ground
1 12-ounce can tomato paste
1 16-ounce can tomatoes, drained and chopped
1½ teaspoons salt
¾ teaspoon pepper
2 small cloves garlic, crushed
1½ teaspoons oregano
1 pound sharp Cheddar cheese, grated

Separate biscuits into three layers. (Each biscuit should make three pizza bites.) Pull across and separate the layers. Place on ungreased baking sheet; prick each roll with a fork. Bake at 300 degrees for 10 minutes or until lightly brown. Put beef into heavy skillet and brown; drain on paper towels and set aside. In saucepan, combine tomato paste, tomatoes and seasonings. Cover and simmer for 10 minutes. Add beef and simmer 10 minutes. Cool. Place one heaping teaspoonful of mixture on each biscuit. Sprinkle with cheese. Bake at 375 degrees for 10 - 15 minutes. Pizza bites may be frozen before baking. Bake frozen ones at 350 degrees for 15-20 minutes. Makes 60. To serve as a main course, do not separate rolls. Place on floured board and roll into 5 inch diameter. Follow method as above. Two to three pizzas make an adequate serving.
Mrs. James Barnett (Lynn)

TANGY WIENERS

"When you don't have time to make meatballs."

3 pounds wieners
1 cup chili sauce
1 cup brown sugar
1 cup bourbon

Cut wieners into bite-size pieces and put into baking dish. Mix remaining ingredients and pour over wieners. Bake covered for 3 hours at 325 degrees. Serve hot in chafing dish. Serves 30.
Mrs. James W. Heacock, Jr. (Harriet)

CHEESE POPCORN

Vegetable oil
Popcorn
1 teaspoon paprika
1 teaspoon salt
⅓ cup cheese, grated

Pour oil, to depth of about ⅛ inch, into pan. Pour enough popcorn into pan to cover bottom one kernel deep. Cover pan tightly and place over high heat. Shake pan when corn begins to pop and continue shaking until corn stops popping. Corn may be popped in electric corn popper. Combine remaining ingredients; sprinkle over hot corn and mix until all popcorn is coated. For more flavor, garlic or onion salt may be substituted for regular salt.
Mrs. Curtis Lackey (Barbara)

BARBECUE DIP

"Men especially love this!"

1 16-ounce jar barbecue sauce
4 chicken breasts, cooked, deboned, and chunked
1 10-ounce jar stuffed olives
2 4-ounce cans cocktail hotdogs or 1 16-ounce package wieners, chunked

Combine all ingredients and put into chafing dish. Jumbo shrimp may also be added. Serve hot.
Mrs. William B. McGehee, III (Evelyn)

CHEESE STRAWS

"A grand addition to a cocktail buffet, a must for a tea."

1 pound sharp New York cheese, grated
½ cup butter
½ teaspoon red pepper
2 cups flour
Salt

Combine cheese and butter; mix to a smooth paste. Sift pepper and flour and work into cheese mixture. Put mixture into cookie press and press on to baking sheets. Sprinkle generously with salt. Bake at 400 degrees until lightly brown.
Mrs. Thomas E. Robbs (Boo)

SWEET-SOUR MEATBALLS

2 pounds beef, ground
1 pound pork, ground
2 cups breadcrumbs, moistened
1 cup beef broth
2 eggs
1 envelope onion soup mix
¼ cup water
2 10-ounce jars currant jelly
2 8-ounce jars brown mustard

Mix all ingredients except mustard and jelly. Make into small balls and brown in skillet. In saucepan, melt jelly over low heat; add mustard and mix until smooth. Place meatballs and sauce into chafing dish and serve hot.
Mrs. G. L. Weaver (Dot)

ASPARAGUS CRISPS

1 pound New York State sharp cheese, grated
2 tablespoons mayonnaise
¼ teaspoon red pepper
Horseradish to taste
1 loaf *very* fresh bread
1 large bell pepper, minced
1 10½-ounce can asparagus tips

Blend first four ingredients. Remove crusts from bread and spread with a thin layer of cheese mixture. Sprinkle with pepper. Place asparagus on edge of bread and roll; fasten with toothpick. Place on broiler pan and toast until brown. Cut in half to serve with cocktails. Leave whole to serve with salad or as luncheon bread. Makes 40 small or 20 large crisps.
Mrs. William B. McGehee, III (Evelyn)

PICKLED SHRIMP

Water
1 cup celery tops
¼ cup pickling spice
3½ tablespoons salt
2½ pounds fresh shrimp, in shells
2 cups onion, sliced
7 or 8 bay leaves
1¼ cup salad oil
¾ cup white vinegar
2½ tablespoons capers
1½ tablespoons salt
2½ tablespoons celery seed
Dash of Tabasco

Cover shrimp with boiling water, add celery tops, pickling spice and salt; simmer five minutes. Drain, peel and clean shrimp under cold water. In a shallow baking dish alternate shrimp, onions and bay leaves. Combine the remainder of ingredients to make a marinade. Mix well and pour over shrimp; cover and chill at least 24 hours. Spoon marinade over shrimp occasionally. Best made 3 days before serving.
Mrs. Julian L. Elliott, Sr. (Margaret)

SEAFOOD MOUSSE

"Fresh shrimp makes this a delight."

2 envelopes plain gelatin
½ cup cold water
3 3-ounce packages cream cheese
1 can cream of tomato soup
1 cup Hellmann's mayonnaise
½ cup celery, finely chopped
½ cup green pepper, finely chopped
½ teaspoon onion juice
1 pound shrimp, cooked or lobster or lump crabmeat

Soak gelatin in water. Heat soup and cream cheese in saucepan until cheese is melted. Add gelatin and mix well. Cool slightly. Add remaining ingredients and mix. Pour into greased salad mold. (Mayonnaise may be used to grease mold.) Refrigerate until congealed, overnight to 24 hours. Unmold on platter and garnish with parsley or slices of hard-cooked eggs and ripe olives. Serve with crackers. Serves 30.
Mrs. James W. Heacock, Jr. (Harriet)
Mrs. N. P. Zauber Pittsburgh, Pennsylvania
Mrs. Freeman Deitz (Miriam)

PICKLED OYSTERS

100 oysters (approximately 4 pints)
1 pint vinegar
1 handful whole peppercorns
6 small red peppers
1 tablespoon whole allspice
2 pieces whole mace
6 or 8 cloves
1 tablespoon salt

Scald oysters in their own juice until they curl slightly. Remove from heat and drain in a sieve saving the liquor. Scald spices in vinegar and pour over the oysters with 1 pint of oyster liquor. Place in sterilized half pint jars. If oysters are large and are not covered by the liquor, add equal parts vinegar and oyster liquor to cover. Seal jars. Chill before serving.
Mrs. W. B. McGehee, Jr. (Mary Lib)

CLAM DIP

"Great with fresh vegetables."

1 8-ounce package cream cheese
1 3-ounce package cream cheese and chives (optional)
1 tablespoon lemon juice, freshly squeezed
½ teaspoon salt
¼ teaspoon pepper
1 tablespoon Worcestershire sauce
1 8-ounce can Doxee clams, minced

Mix all ingredients except clams. Beat with mixer until smooth. Drain clams, reserving juice. Slowly add clams to mixture and stir enough to mix. Add juice to desired consistency. More lemon juice or Worcestershire sauce may be added for more flavor. Refrigerate. Let stand at room temperature 30 minutes before serving. Serves 10-12.
Mrs. Wallis Elliott (Dede)

ARTICHOKE APPETIZER

1 14-ounce can artichoke hearts
½ cup mayonnaise
1 cup Parmesan cheese
Garlic salt to taste

Pull artichokes apart and drain; set aside. Mix other ingredients thoroughly. Add artichokes and stir. Place in baking dish; bake at 350 degrees for 20-25 minutes or until bubbles form. Serve hot on crackers. Can be made ahead and refrigerated prior to baking.
Mrs. William Lawrence (Sally)

CHAFING DISH MEATBALLS

2 pounds beef, ground
1 egg, slightly beaten
1 large onion, grated
Salt to taste
1 12-ounce bottle chili sauce
Juice of 1 lemon
½ 16-ounce jar grape jelly

Mix first four ingredients and shape into small balls. In saucepan, combine chili sauce, lemon juice and jelly and simmer for several minutes. Add meatballs and continue to simmer until brown. Serve in chafing dish. Makes 50-60 meatballs.
Mrs. Jack Wright (Joyce)

QUICHE LORRAINE TARTS

1 package Betty Crocker pie crust mix
1½ cups Swiss cheese, grated
⅔ cup bacon, crumbled
½ cup onion, chopped
4 eggs, slightly beaten
1 cup sour cream
1 teaspoon salt
1 teaspoon Worcestershire sauce

Prepare pastry according to package directions. Roll pastry 1/16 inch thick and cut into 2½ inch rounds. Place rounds into small muffin tins. Combine cheese, bacon and onions; spoon into pastry tarts. Stir together eggs, sour cream, salt and Worcestershire sauce. Pour approximately one tablespoonfull sour cream mixture on top of cheese mixture. Bake at 375 degrees for 25 minutes. Cool 5 minutes before serving. Can be made ahead and warmed in aluminum foil for 10 minutes at 350 degrees. Makes 36 tarts.
Mrs. James W. Heacock, Jr. (Harriet)

SPINACH DIP

"Good with vegetables or chips – it's different!"

1 10-ounce package frozen spinach, chopped
1 3-ounce package cream cheese
1 cup mayonnaise
3 small green onions, chopped finely
2 to 4 tablespoons parsley flakes
Salt to taste

Thaw spinach; drain well, squeezing dry with hands. Add remaining ingredients. Mix well. Makes 2 cups.
Mrs. Hugo Molliston (Marion)

CURRIED TUNA APPETIZERS

1 7-ounce can tuna, drained
¼ teaspoon salt
½ teaspoon curry powder
3 tablespoons mayonnaise
1 teaspoon lemon juice
2 teaspoons instant minced onion
Dash of Tabasco (optional)
Pimento strips (optional)
6 crepes, cooked

Break tuna into small pieces. Add salt, curry powder, mayonnaise, lemon juice, onion and Tabasco. Spread on crepes; roll up. Refrigerate until serving time. Cut each crepe into 4 pieces. Garnish with pimento strips. Makes 24.
Mrs. Jay Thornton (Willene)

TRIO-CHEESE BALL

1 8-ounce package cream cheese, softened
4 ounces blue cheese
4 ounces sharp Cheddar cheese, grated
1 small onion, grated
1 tablespoon Worcestershire sauce
1 cup pecans, chopped or 1 cup parsley, chopped

Mix all ingredients together by hand; form into ball. Roll in pecans or parsley. Chill at least 2 hours before serving with crackers.
Mrs. Cleve Jacobs (Patti)
Variation: 1 tablespoon sherry may be added. *Mrs. Robert Mullins (JoAnn)*

FINGER DRUMSTICKS

1½ pounds (12 - 15) chicken wings
Salt
Pepper
1 cup chicken bouillon
¼ cup sugar
¼ teaspoon ginger
⅛ teaspoon garlic salt
1 tablespoon cornstarch
½ teaspoon salt
⅛ teaspoon pepper
2 tablespoons soy sauce
3 tablespoons lemon juice

Cut off and discard wing tips; divide each wing at joint. Sprinkle meat with salt and pepper and put into crockpot. Pour bouillon over meat; cover and cook on low 4 - 5 hours or until tender. Drain. In small saucepan, combine remaining ingredients and simmer; stir occasionally until mixture thickens slightly. Place chicken on broiler pan; brush with sauce and brown under broiler. Turn meat and repeat. Return meat to crockpot and serve hot. Makes 25-30 drumsticks.
Mrs. Herb Studebaker *Jesup, Georgia*

SPINACH STUFFED MUSHROOMS

"A starter or a meal treat."

12 large mushrooms or 1 pound small mushrooms
3 tablespoons butter, melted
⅛ teaspoon garlic powder
1 10-ounce package frozen spinach, chopped
3 tablespoons Hellmann's mayonnaise
3 tablespoons Parmesan cheese, grated
Dash Tabasco
2 tablespoons lemon juice
½ teaspoon Worcestershire sauce
1 teaspoon salt

Remove stems of mushrooms. Wash caps and dry well. Mix butter and garlic powder. Dip each cap into mixture and place in greased flat casserole dish. Cook spinanch by directions on package. Drain spinach well; add remaining ingredients and mix thoroughly. Fill caps with mixture. Bake at 350 degrees for 20 minutes or until heated through. Serves 6 when used as a meal vegetable.
Mrs. James W. Heacock, Jr. (Harriet)

CHEESE-OLIVE BALLS

1 5-ounce package bacon-cheese spread
4 tablespoons margarine
Dash hot pepper sauce
Dash Worcestershire sauce
¾ cup all-purpose flour, sifted
1 5-ounce jar stuffed green olives

Blend cheese and margarine until light and fluffy. Add sauces and mix well. Stir in flour. Shape dough around olives, using one teaspoonful. Place on ungreased baking sheet. Bake at 400 degrees for 12-15 minutes. May be made ahead and refrigerated before baking. Serve warm. Makes 3 dozen.
Mrs. William Hurst, Jr. (Sandra)

VEGETABLE DIP

1 cup mayonnaise
2 teaspoons tarragon vinegar
Salt to taste
Pepper to taste
¼ teaspoon curry powder
¼ teaspoon thyme
2 tablespoons chili sauce
1 teaspoon onion juice

Mix all ingredients. Chill. Better if made day before serving. Serve with fresh vegetables.
Mrs. James W. Heacock, Jr. (Harriet)
Similar recipe submitted by Mrs. Cleve Jacobs (Patti)

MINIATURE PARTY PUFFS

1 cup boiling water
½ cup margarine
1 cup self-rising flour
Dash salt
4 eggs

Stir margarine in water until melted. Add flour and salt; stir well. Cool slightly. Add eggs, one at a time, beating well after each addition. Continue to beat until mixture is shiny. Drop by teaspoonsful onto lightly greased baking sheet. Bake at 375 degrees for 40 minutes. When cool, cut hole in top of puff and fill with desired salad as chicken, shrimp, or tuna. Makes 45 puffs.
Mrs. Carl Reaves (Joyce)

CHEESE BISCUITS

1¼ cup flour
Dash salt
Dash cayenne pepper
6 tablespoons butter
1 cup Cheddar cheese, grated
6 tablespoons heavy cream
1 egg, slightly beaten
1 cup Swiss cheese, grated
2 tablespoons butter

Sift flour, salt and pepper. Add butter and Cheddar cheese; mix until mixture resembles meal. Stir in cream and form a ball. Chill several hours. Roll out dough and cut into 2-inch circles. Brush rounds with egg; place on greased baking sheet. Bake at 450 degrees for 6-8 minutes or until brown. Cream Swiss cheese and butter; spread on one half of rounds. Cover with remaining rounds and return to oven. Bake until biscuits are heated throughout. Good as hors d' oeuvres or served with lunch. Makes 20 biscuits.
Mrs. William B. McGehee, Jr. (Mary Lib)

CRAB-STUFFED MUSHROOMS

"This marvel on your table means sure party success."

12 large mushrooms
2 tablespoons salad oil
1 6-ounce package frozen crabmeat, thawed and drained
1 egg, lightly beaten
2 tablespoons mayonnaise
2 tablespoons onion, chopped
1 teaspoon lemon juice
½ cup soft bread crumbs, divided
2 tablespoons butter, melted

Clean mushrooms; remove stems and brush caps with oil. Place in buttered baking dish. Combine crabmeat, egg, mayonnaise, onion, lemon juice, and half of bread crumbs. Stuff caps with mixture. Combine remaining bread crumbs with butter and sprinkle over caps. Bake at 375 degrees for 15 minutes. Serves 6.
Mrs. Larkin Coker (Joan)

MARINATED MUSHROOMS

"These are as easy to pop in your mouth as to prepare."

1 pound fresh whole mushroom caps
½ cup salad oil
½ cup vinegar
2 tablespoons onion, finely chopped
2 tablespoons parsley, finely chopped
2 cloves garlic, crushed
½ teaspoon salt
½ teaspoon sugar

Wash caps well and place in skillet with small amount of butter; sauté until slightly brown. Mix remaining ingredients. Place caps in marinade; coat well. Refrigerate at least 12 hours before serving. Drain mushrooms well and serve with toothpicks.
Mrs. Jack Edmiston (Candy)

CHEESE DIP

1 20-ounce can tomatoes, drained
1 clove garlic, minced
1 medium onion, chopped
1 4-ounce can green chili peppers, chopped
1 pound Velveeta cheese, diced

Combine all ingredients except cheese in saucepan. Cook over high heat until all juice is gone. Add cheese and stir until melted. Serve hot with triangle crackers. May be made ahead and reheated.
Mrs. John Barksdale (Dorothy)

HOT CRABMEAT DIP

1 8-ounce package cream cheese, softened
1 tablespoon milk
1 7-ounce can crabmeat, drained
3 tablespoons onion, chopped
½ teaspoon horseradish
¼ teaspoon salt
Dash pepper
⅓ cup almonds, sliced

Blend cream cheese with milk until smooth. Add remaining ingredients except almonds and mix well. Pour into baking dish. Sprinkle with almonds and bake at 350 degrees for 20 minutes. Serve hot with party rye or Melba toast.
Mrs. Jack Anderson Decatur, Georgia

SALMON PARTY LOG

"A marvelous recipe for the Yule Season."

1 16-ounce can salmon
1 8-ounce package cream cheese, softened
1 tablespoon lemon juice
2 teaspoons onions, grated
1 teaspoon horseradish
¼ teaspoon salt
¼ teaspoon liquid smoke
¼ cup pecans, chopped
3 tablespoons parsley, snipped

Drain and flake salmon, removing skin and bones. Combine with next six ingredients; mix thoroughly. Chill several hours. Combine pecans and parsley. Shape salmon mixture into 8 x 2-inch log and roll in nut mixture. Chill well. Serve with crackers.
Mrs. Tony McKinney (Jeanne)
Mrs. E. L. Tibbits (Emma Lee)

BROCCOLI DIP

½ stick margarine
1 tablespoon onion, chopped
2 cans cream of mushroom soup
2 5-ounce rolls garlic cheese, diced
2 10-ounce packages frozen broccoli, cooked, chopped and drained
1 3-ounce can mushrooms, sliced
Rye croutons (optional)

Sauté onion in margarine. Add soup and blend well. Add cheese and stir until melted. Add broccoli and mushrooms and mix well. Pour into baking dish. Garnish with rye croutons and bake at 350 degrees for 25-30 minutes. Serve hot with crackers. May be served as a **casserole** by using 1 can soup and 1 roll of cheese.
Mrs. John Sartain (Linda)

DRIED BEEF APPETIZER

"A sure hit – especially with the men!"

1 4-ounce package cream cheese
1 package Frito dried green onion dip
Mayonnaise to spread
1 3-ounce jar dried beef

Combine all ingredients except dried beef; mix well. Spread mixture on dried beef and roll like jelly roll. Freeze. Remove from freezer; slice and thaw at least 30 minutes before serving. May also be served whole.
Mrs. James Luker (Judy)

CHICKEN APPETIZERS

1 3-ounce package cream cheese, softened
1 5-ounce can chicken spread
½ cup chopped apple
¼ cup chopped walnuts
2 tablespoons chopped parsley
½ teaspoon Worcestershire sauce
Dash cayenne pepper
Wheat germ

In a bowl stir cream cheese until smooth; blend in the remaining ingredients except for the wheat germ. Chill. Shape into small balls and roll in wheat germ. Makes 38 appetizers.
Mrs. Ken H. Wallis (Kathy)

ANCHOVY PUFFS

½ cup margarine
1 3-ounce package cream cheese
1 cup flour
Anchovy paste

Blend margarine and cream cheese. Mix with flour and chill. Roll very thin and cut with 2-inch biscuit cutter. Spread with thin layer anchovy paste and fold over. Bake at 400 degrees for 10 minutes. Serve hot. Makes 50.
Mrs. James W. Heacock, Jr. (Harriet)

CRABMEAT A LA MORNAY

1 stick butter
1 small bunch onions, chopped
2 tablespoons flour
1 pint half and half
¼ pound Swiss cheese, grated
¼ pound Cheddar cheese, grated
½ cup parsley, chopped
1 tablespoon sherry wine
Red pepper and salt to taste
½ pound fresh shrimp, cooked
½ pound fresh or canned white crabmeat

Melt butter in heavy pot and sauté onions. Blend in flour, cream and cheese until cheese is melted. Add other ingredients and gently fold in shrimp and crabmeat. Serve in chafing dish with Melba Toast rounds or in patty shells. Serves 20.
Mrs. Stan Thornton (Cathy)
Mrs. Will Lawrence (Sally)

CHEESE DELIGHTS

½ pound New York cheese, grated
2 sticks margarine, softened
⅛ teaspoon red pepper
1 scant teaspoon salt
3¼ cups plain flour
½ cup nuts, finely chopped

Mix cheese and margarine. Add pepper, salt, and flour; mix well. Add nuts. Roll into small balls. Place on ungreased baking sheet and flatten with fork. Bake at 350 degrees until slightly brown.
Mrs. James Montgomery (Ann)
Variations: 2 cups Rice Krispies may be used instead of nuts.
Mrs. Alden Limbaugh (Bobbie)
1 envelope onion soup mix may be substituted for red pepper and nuts.
Mrs. John Barksdale (Dorothy)

beverages

PINK CONFETTI PUNCH

"Delicious as beverage or light dessert."

2 ripe bananas, mashed
Juice 2 medium oranges
Juice 2 medium lemons
¼ cup maraschino cherries
1½ cups sugar
1 cup milk
1 cup water
3 tablespoons cherry juice
1 to 1½ 28-ounce bottle ginger ale

Combine bananas and fruit juices. Add remaining ingredients except ginger ale. Mix well. Pour into 9 x 5 x 3-inch loaf pan; cover and freeze until firm. Remove from freezer and beat with mixer until fluffy and pale pink throughout. Pour into covered plastic container; return to freezer and freeze until firm. Allow to mellow at least 24 hours. Several hours prior to serving, remove from freezer; place into punch bowl and add ginger ale just before serving. This may also be served as sherbet omitting ginger ale. Serves 15-20.

Mrs. Charles Nelson (Mary)

HOT APPLE CIDER

"Nothing better on a cold Winter evening"

½ cup brown sugar
¼ teaspoon salt
2 quarts apple cider
12 whole cloves
1 stick cinnamon

Combine sugar, salt, and cider in large saucepan. Do Not Use Aluminum Pan. Put spices in cheese cloth and tie with string. Add to cider. Slowly bring to boil. Reduce heat; cover and simmer. Serve hot.
Mrs. E. H. Gentry (Mary)

HOT CHOCOLATE MIX

1 16-ounce jar non-dairy creamer
1 8-quart box instant nonfat dry milk
1 cup powdered sugar
1 2-pound can instant chocolate drink mix

Mix all ingredients together. Using 3 heaping tablespoons for 1 cup hot water. Store in tight container. Makes one gallon.
Miss Nancy Hanks
Similar recipe submitted by:
Mrs. James Peeple (Mary Frances),
Mrs. Robert Mullins (JoAnn)

EGG NOG

"Perfect for that special occasion"

14 eggs, separated
1 pint whiskey
14 tablespoons sugar
1 quart and ½ pint cream, whipped

Place egg yolks in mixing bowl and beat. Add whiskey very slowly, a teaspoon at a time. Increase additions by small amounts, beating continually until all whiskey and egg yolks are combined. Add sugar slowly. Whip cream and add slowly. Beat egg whites until stiff and fold into mixture.
Mrs. Turner Jones (Katherine)

WASSAIL PUNCH
"A Christmas Must"

1 gallon apple cider
1 quart orange juice
1 cup lemon juice
1 quart pineapple juice
24 whole cloves
4 sticks cinnamon
1 cup sugar

Combine all ingredients and simmer for 10 minutes. Remove cinnamon and cloves. Serve warm in punch cups. Yield: 1½ gallons.
Mrs. William Hurst, Jr. (Sandra)

HOMEMADE GRAPE WINE

1 package dry yeast
1 cup warm water
18 ounces frozen grape juice
4¼ cups sugar
Water

Dissolve yeast in warm water. Thaw juice and add to yeast mixture. Add sugar and mix well. Pour into one gallon jug. Add water to just below neck of jug. Place balloon over top of jug. Put in very warm place for 21 days.
Mrs. Toby Deese (Ruth Helen)

ICED COFFEE PUNCH

2 cups water
1¾ cups sugar
1 2-ounce jar instant coffee
1 gallon milk
½ or 1 gallon vanilla ice cream

Bring water and sugar to a boil; add the coffee and cover. Steep until the mixture is cool and then add milk. Just before serving, add broken-up ice cream into punch bowl and pour mixture over it. Serves 50.
Mrs. Danny Harris (Joan)

LIME PUNCH

"Do ahead and freeze."

5 3-ounce packages lime jello
5 cups hot water
1 20-ounce can crushed pineapple
1 20-ounce can grapefruit juice
2 quarts pineapple juice
5 cups sugar
1 16-ounce bottle lemon juice or juice 2½ dozen lemons
5½ quarts water
6 to 8 quarts ginger ale

Dissolve jello in water. Mix pineapple, juices, sugar, and water. Add jello and mix well. Put in milk cartons and freeze. Remove from freezer several hours before ready to serve. Place in punch bowl and add ginger ale.
Mrs. Gordon T. Welch (Marietta)

MULLED WINE

¾ cup light brown sugar
1 quart cranberry juice
2 tablespoons lemon juice
4 cinnamon sticks
2½ teaspoons whole cloves
2½ cups Burgundy
1 lemon, sliced

Put all ingredients except Burgundy into large saucepan. Bring to boil. Boil, uncovered, for 5 minutes. Remove from heat. Add Burgundy and lemon slices. Cover and let stand 10 minutes. Remove cloves and cinnamon sticks. Serve in mugs.
Mrs. Michael Reeves (Susan)

BUNCH PUNCH

1 fifth Southern Comfort bourbon
1 6-ounce can frozen lemonade
1 6-ounce can frozen orange juice
3 quarts 7-Up, chilled
6 thin slices lemon
6 thin slices orange

Combine all ingredients in punch bowl. Add ice or ice ring made with fruit juice. Stir well and serve. Serves 30.
Mrs. David Newman (Frankie)

INSTANT RUSSIAN TEA

2 cups Tang
2½ cups sugar
1 cup instant tea
1 package lemonade mix
1 teaspoon cinnamon
½ teaspoon ground cloves

Mix all ingredients together thoroughly and put into a tightly closed container. Use 2 to 3 heaping teaspoons of mixture for each cup hot water. Will keep up to six months. Yield 25-30 cups.
Mrs. Gordon Herring (Maxine)

HOT PERKED PUNCH

1 quart cranberry juice
1 quart unsweetened pineapple juice
½ quart water
1 cup brown sugar
1 teaspoon whole cloves
1 teaspoon whole allspice
1 lemon, sliced
2 sticks cinnamon

Pour first three ingredients into large coffee pot. Pour remaining ingredients into basket of coffee pot. Perk as if making coffee. Makes 15 cups.
Mrs. Tommy Fite (Betty)

soups

CHICKEN GUMBO SOUP

"A flavorful stew – a specialty of Creole cuisine."

3½ to 4 pound hen or fryer
1 cup celery stems and leaves, chopped
Salt to taste
3 medium potatoes, diced
2 large onions, chopped
2 cups okra, diced
1 cup carrots, diced
2 cups tomatoes
1 10-ounce package frozen baby green butter beans
2 cups tomato juice
¼ teaspoon pepper
1 tablespoon Worcestershire sauce
2 ears fresh corn, scraped or 1 8½-ounce can cream-style corn

Place chicken in large saucepan and fill with water until chicken is half covered. Add celery and salt. Cook until chicken is tender. Place remaining vegetables except corn in large saucepan; add tomato juice and enough water to cover. Cook over low heat. When chicken is done, remove and cut into bite-size pieces. Add chicken, broth, seasonings, and corn to vegetables and continue to simmer; stir occasionally to prevent sticking. Preparation time 1½-2 hours.

Mrs. John Coleman (Mary Dowdell)

BRUNSWICK STEW

"A crowd pleaser – great for cookouts!"

3 3-4 pound boston butts, cooked and chunked
4 whole chickens, cooked and chunked
8 16-ounce cans tomatoes, drained and mashed
12 16-ounce cans cream-style corn
6 16-ounce cans white corn
6 16-ounce cans green lima beans
4 pounds frozen okra, sliced
1 gallon chicken broth
3 32-ounce bottles catsup
5 pounds potatoes, finely diced
3 large onions, finely diced
1 tablespoon prepared mustard
4 teaspoons turmeric
4 teaspoons ground cumin
1 10-ounce bottle Worcestershire sauce
1 cup tomato juice
Tabasco to taste
Salt to taste
Pepper to taste

Cook and prepare meats, reserving chicken broth. Drain and mash tomatoes, reserving juice. In a very large cooking pan, combine all ingredients and mix well. Add reserved liquids to stew, as needed, during cooking. Cook over very low heat for 12-18 hours. Cooking time may vary according to taste. Serves 100.

Mrs. James Barnett (Lynn)
Mrs. David Newman (Frankie)
Mr. Jesse Foshee

CHICKEN SOUP

3½ quarts water
1 3¼-pounds fryer chicken, whole
3 sprigs parsley
Salt
2 chicken bouillon cubes
2 cups carrots, diced
2 cups celery, diced
1 medium onion, sliced
½ teaspoon pepper
1 5-ounce package medium noodles

Place water, chicken, parsley, and salt in large saucepan and heat to boiling. Cover; reduce heat and simmer one hour or until chicken is tender. Remove chicken. Strain broth and return to pan. Add bouillon cubes and boil. Add vegetables and pepper; cover and continue cooking for 5 minutes. Add noodles; continue to cook, stirring occasionally until noodles are tender. Cut chicken into bite-size pieces, discarding skin and bones. Add to soup and heat 5 minutes longer.

Mrs. Kenneth Barnes (Connie)

EGG DROP SOUP

2 eggs, beaten
2 teaspoons water
1 tablespoon cornstarch
3 tablespoons water
6 cups rich chicken stock
½ teaspoon sugar
¾ to 1 teaspoon salt
1 teaspoon sherry
1 tablespoon soy sauce
2 scallions, minced

Combine eggs and water. In bowl blend cornstarch and water to form paste. Pour chicken stock into large saucepan and bring to boil. Reduce heat to medium and add remaining ingredients. Add cornstarch paste and cook soup until thickened and smooth. Reduce heat to low. Pour eggs in slowly, stirring constantly until they separate into shreds. Turn off heat. Garnish with scallions and serve hot. May be prepared in advance but don't add eggs until ready to heat and serve. Serves 6-8.
Mrs. Nelson G. Conover (Muffett)

FRENCH ONION SOUP

5 cups onion, sliced
3 tablespoons butter
1 tablespoon oil
1 teaspoon sugar
3 tablespoons flour
½ gallon beef broth, bouillon or canned broth may be used
½ cup white wine

Sauté onions in butter and oil for 15 minutes over low heat. Add sugar and stir constantly for 5 more minutes. Add flour and stir 5 minutes. Add beef broth and simmer 2 hours. Add wine and serve with croutons and Parmesan or Gruyere cheese. Freezes beautifully.
Mrs. William B. McGehee, III (Evelyn)

NEW ENGLAND CLAM CHOWDER

"A New England restaurant recipe."

2 cans cream potato soup
1 can cream celery soup
2 soup cans milk
2 8-ounce cans clams, minced and drained
½ small onion, minced

Mix all ingredients together in a saucepan and heat. Quick and easy and great with sandwiches.

Mrs. J. L. Perry *Spartanburg, South Carolina*

SUMMER SQUASH SOUP

2 medium yellow squash, chopped
2 small green zucchini squash, chopped
1½ cups celery leaves
3 tablespoons butter
2 cans Swanson's chicken broth
Salt to taste
Celery salt to taste
Pepper to taste
2 tablespoons parsley, chopped

Place squash, celery leaves, and butter in saucepan and cook over low heat until tender. Place mixture in blender and puree, adding a small amount of chicken broth. Add remaining chicken broth and seasonings. Garnish with parsley or croutons and serve hot or cold. Serves 6.

Mrs. C. L. Kelley (Hattie)

VEGETABLE CHOWDER

2½ cups boiling water
2 cups potatoes, diced
¾ cup onions, diced
½ cup celery, diced
1½ teaspoons salt
4 tablespoons margarine, melted
4 tablespoons flour
¼ teaspoon pepper
½ teaspoon dry mustard
1½ teaspoons salt
2 cups milk
¼ pound Cheddar cheese, grated
1 16-ounce can tomatoes, drained
1 tablespoon parsley, chopped

Mix first five ingredients together in saucepan and simmer until tender. Combine next six ingredients in another saucepan and cook until thick. Add cheese and stir until melted. Add potato mixture, tomatoes, and parsley and mix well. Serves 8.

Miss Toni and Miss Nora Hardiman *Birmingham, Alabama*

NEVER FAIL CRAB-GUMBO

- 2 tablespoons lard
- 2 tablespoons flour
- 2 medium onions, chopped
- 4 celery stalks, chopped
- 1 bell pepper, chopped
- 2 20-ounce cans tomatoes
- ½ pound okra, sliced
- 3 quarts water
- 1 pound raw shrimp, cleaned
- 1 pound crabmeat
- 1 teaspoon salt
- Black pepper to taste
- Red pepper to taste
- Tabasco sauce to taste
- 2 bay leaves

Make a roux in heavy skillet of lard and flour. Stir in onions, celery, and pepper and simmer a few minutes. Add tomatoes and okra; simmer until okra is tender. Place in large saucepan. Add water, shrimp, crabmeat, and seasonings and cook slowly over low heat for several hours. The longer it cooks the better. Gumbo is even better the next day. Serve in soup bowls over steaming hot rice.
Mr. Larkin Coker

GAZPACHO (COLD SOUP)

"For a Spanish treat."

- 7 slices white bread, cut each into 4 pieces
- 1 quart water
- 4 large tomatoes, peeled and diced
- 2 cloves garlic
- ¼ cup olive oil
- 3 tablespoons vinegar
- 1 tablespoon salt
- ⅛ teaspoon white pepper
- ½ medium cucumber, diced
- 1 small bell pepper, chopped
- 2 hard boiled egg yolks
- 8 ice cubes

Soak bread in water 10 minutes. Remove bread and place into a large bowl. Add remaining ingredients except ice cubes. Place one third of mixture into blender, adding some of the water in which bread was soaked. Beat until smooth. Repeat with remaining mixture. Add ice cubes and beat until dissolved. Refrigerate at least 2 hours before serving. Garnish soup with small pieces of vegetables, white of eggs, and croutons. Serves 10-12.
Mrs. Russell Wells (Janis)

Purefoy Gazebo
by Connie Barnes

Breads

bread

TOP HAT COFFEE CAKE

"Perfect for a morning coffee."

½ cup margarine
1 cup sugar
2 eggs
1 cup sour cream
1 teaspoon vanilla
2 cups cake flour or all-purpose flour
1 teaspoon baking powder
1 teaspoon baking soda
½ teaspoon salt
⅔ cup light brown sugar, packed
1 tablespoon cinnamon
2 tablespoons margarine, melted
1 cup pecans, chopped

Cream together margarine and sugar. Add eggs, sour cream, and vanilla; beat well. Sift together flour, baking powder, soda, and salt. Add to creamed mixture; blending well. Pour half of mixture into ungreased tube pan or 9 x 13 x 2-inch pan. Mix brown sugar, cinnamon, margarine, and nuts. Cover mixture with one half of topping. Add remaining batter and topping. Bake 350 degrees 55-60 minutes for tube pan or 40-45 minutes for 9 x 13 x 2-inch pan.

Mrs. Byron Boyett (Margaret)
Similar recipes submitted by:
Mrs. Tony McKinney (Jeanne)
Mrs. Lyle Shepler *Montgomery, Alabama*

CREOLE DOUGHNUTS

"This recipe was brought to Louisiana by wives of French Soldiers."

2 cups milk, scalded
1 package dry yeast
¼ cup warm water
½ cup sugar
½ cup cooking oil
1½ teaspoons salt
7 cups flour, sifted
2 eggs, beaten

In saucepan, scald milk. Soften yeast in water; let stand 5 minutes. Put into large bowl sugar, oil, and salt. Add scalded milk; cool to lukewarm. Add one cup of flour and beat until smooth. Add yeast mixture and mix well. Add remaining flour and beat until smooth. Add eggs, one third at a time and beat after each addition. Add enough flour to make dough soft. Turn onto floured surface and allow to rest 5-10 minutes. Knead dough; form into smooth ball and place in greased bowl with greased surface on top. Cover with waxpaper and towel and let stand in warm place until dough is doubled (1½-2 hours). Punch down dough. Turn onto floured surface and roll ¼ inch thick. Cut into 2-inch squares or diamonds or use doughnut cutter. Place on floured board; cover and let rise in warm place until double. About 20 minutes before deep fat frying, fill a deep saucepan ½-⅔ full of shortening. Heat to 365 degrees. Fry 2-3 minutes or until brown. (Do Not Crowd.) Drain on paper towels. Shake in a bag filled with confectioners' sugar, if desired. Serve warm. Store in tightly covered container.
Mrs. Ray Miller (Marianne)

MARSHMALLOW CRESCENT PUFFS

"A real treat for breakfast or dessert."

¼ cup sugar
1 teaspoon cinnamon
2 8-ounce cans Crescent dinner rolls
16 large marshmallows
¼ cup margarine, melted
½ cup powdered sugar
½ teaspoon vanilla
2 to 3 teaspoons milk
¼ cup nuts, chopped

Combine sugar and cinnamon. Separate dough into 16 triangles. Dip marshmallow into margarine, sugar mixture, and place on dough. Wrap and squeeze edges to seal. Dip in margarine and place buttered side down in muffin tin. Repeat with remaining marshmallows. Bake at 375 degrees for 10-15 minutes or until brown. Mix powdered sugar, vanilla, and milk and drizzle on puffs. Sprinkle with nuts. May be made ahead and refrigerated for 2-3 hours prior to baking. Makes 16 puffs.
Mrs. Larry Edmiston (Donna)

MARMALADE ROLLS

"Really worth your effort."

½ cup warm water
1 package dry yeast
1 egg
1 tablespoon sugar
2½ cups Bisquick
4 tablespoons butter
¾ to 1 cup orange marmalade

Dissolve yeast in warm water. Add egg, sugar, and Bisquick; beat vigorously. Turn out onto well dusted surface, using Bisquick and knead until smooth (about 20 times). Place ½ teaspoon soft butter and ½ teaspoon marmalade in each of 12 greased muffin tins. Roll dough into 16 x 9-inch rectangle; spread with remaining butter and marmalade. Roll up tightly beginning at wide side. Seal by pinching edge of dough. Cut into 12 slices. Place into prepared cups; cover with a damp cloth. Let rise in warm place about 45 minutes. Bake for 15 minutes in 400 degree oven. Invert pan on rack or baking sheet. Serve warm. Freezes well. Makes 12 rolls.

Mrs. Allen G. McMillan, Jr. (Jean)

COFFEE NUT CAKE

"Be sure to try this breakfast cake. It's wonderful!"

2 tablespoons margarine, melted
⅔ cup dark corn syrup
⅔ cup brown sugar
⅔ cup pecans, chopped
3 cups biscuit mix
⅓ cup sugar
1 cup evaporated milk
2 tablespoons water

Grease 9 x 9 x 2-inch baking dish. Mix margarine, syrup, sugar, and pecans and spread evenly over bottom of dish. Combine biscuit mix and sugar in a bowl; stir in milk and water enough to moisten ingredients. Spread over nut mixture. Bake at 350 degrees for 35-40 minutes or until center is done. Let cool 5-10 minutes and turn from dish. Serve warm with Cool Whip, if desired. Serves 8-10.

Mrs. Joe Woodard (Jerry)

OLD FASHIONED STICKY BUNS

"These are superb! Don't fail to try them."

¾ cup 40% Bran Flakes, finely crushed
¼ cup brown sugar, packed
¼ cup raisins
1 teaspoon cinnamon
1 8-ounce can biscuits
2 tablespoons margarine,melted
¼ cup Log Cabin Syrup

Combine cereal, sugar, raisins, and cinnamon and set aside. On a lightly floured board, overlap biscuits in two rows to form a rectangle; pinch edges together. Roll to measure 6 x 10-inches. Brush with margarine and sprinkle with ¼ cup cereal mixture. Roll lengthwise and cut into 10 slices. Place 1 inch apart on a greased 8-inch layer pan. Drizzle with syrup and remaining margarine. Sprinkle with remaining cereal mixture. Bake at 450 degrees for 15 minutes or until brown. Invert on plate; remove pan. Makes 10 buns.

Mrs. Randall Stewart (Reba)

BRAN MUFFINS

"A nice change from ordinary muffins."

2 cups boiling water
2 cups 100% Bran
1 cup shortening
3 cups sugar
4 eggs, beaten
5 cups flour
5 teaspoons soda
1 teaspoon salt
1 quart buttermilk
4 cups All-Bran

Mix water and bran and set aside. Cream shortening and sugar; add eggs and mix. Add bran mixture. Sift together flour, soda, and salt and add alternately with buttermilk. Fold in All-Bran and mix only until moistened. Grease and lightly flour muffin tins; fill ¾ full. Bake at 400 degrees for 15-20 minutes. Makes one gallon of mixture. Will keep six weeks in refrigerator.

Ms. Jean Thornton

Variation: 1 cup raisins may be added.

Mrs. James Harris (Nettie)

Mrs. Wayne Grant   Atlanta, Georgia

HOMEMADE CINNAMON ROLLS

2 cups flour
2 teaspoons baking powder
¼ teaspoon soda
¾ teaspoon salt
¼ cup shortening
⅔ cup buttermilk
1 stick margarine
½ cup sugar
Cinnamon
½ box confectioners' sugar
¼ cup milk

Sift together dry ingredients. Cut in shortening until coarse like cornmeal. Stir in buttermilk until dough is soft. Roll out dough until very thin. Dot with margarine. Sprinkle with sugar and cinnamon. Roll dough, as for jelly roll, and cut into ¾ inch slices. Place on greased cookie sheet. Bake at 450 degrees for 15 minutes or until brown. Mix confectioners' sugar with milk and glaze rolls.
Mrs. Toby Deese (Ruth Helen)

DILLY CASSEROLE BREAD

"Everyone who tastes it – loves it."

1 package dry yeast
¼ cup warm water
1 cup cream cottage cheese
2 tablespoons sugar
1 teaspoon instant minced onion
1 teaspoon margarine
2 teaspoons dill seed
1 teaspoon salt
¼ teaspoon soda
1 egg
2¼ to 2½ cups plain flour

Soften yeast in warm water. Heat cottage cheese until lukewarm. In mixing bowl, combine all ingredients except flour. Gradually add flour to mixture, to make a soft dough, beating well after each addition. Let rise until double (about one hour). Stir down and turn into well greased 1½ to 2-quart round casserole dish. Let rise in warm place 30-40 minutes. Bake 350 degrees for 40-50 minutes or until golden brown. Brush with margarine and sprinkle with salt.
Mrs. Fred Hughston (Pat)

MUFFINS TROPICALE

"They are scrumptious."

2 cups all-purpose flour
2 teaspoons baking powder
½ teaspoon baking soda
½ teaspoon salt
½ cup brown sugar, packed
1 egg, beaten
1 cup sour cream
1 8¾-ounce can crushed pineapple, undrained
½ cup pecans, chopped
⅓ cup cooking oil

Mix together dry ingredients. Combine egg and sour cream. Add pineapple, nuts, and oil. Add to dry ingredients and stir until moistened. Fill greased or paper lined muffin tins ⅔ full. Bake at 400 degrees about 20 minutes. For a sweeter muffin, more sugar may be added. Makes 18 muffins.

Mrs. Walter Burt (Brenda)

QUICK MUFFINS

"Win the mother-of-the-day award with these for breakfast."

1 cup sugar
½ cup margarine
2 eggs
1¾ cups flour, sifted
2 teaspoons baking powder
½ cup milk
1 teaspoon vanilla

Cream sugar and margarine. Add eggs, one at a time, beating well after each. Sift flour; measure; add baking powder and sift again. Add flour alternately with milk. Add vanilla. Pour into muffin tins lined with paper bake cups. Bake at 350 degrees until done, about 15 minutes. For a variation, 1 cup blueberries may be added. Makes 18 muffins.

Mrs. John Q. Adams (Sara)

CRANBERRY FRUIT NUT BREAD

"Perfect for holiday get togethers."

2 cups all-purpose flour, sifted
1 cup sugar
1½ teaspoons baking powder
1 teaspoon salt
½ teaspoon baking soda
¼ cup shortening
1 teaspoon orange peel, grated
¾ cup orange juice
1 egg, beaten
1 cup fresh cranberries, coarsely chopped
½ cup nuts, chopped

Sift together dry ingredients. Cut in shortening. Combine peel, juice, and egg. Add to dry ingredients, mixing just to moisten. Fold in berries and nuts. Turn into greased 9x5x3 inch pan. Bake for one hour at 350 degrees. Cool. Wrap and store overnight.

Mrs. Crawford Nelson (Linda)

BANANA BREAD

"For a different flavor."

1/3 cup shortening
2/3 cup sugar
2 eggs
1/4 cup milk
3/4 teaspoon vinegar
1 cup banana, mashed
1 cup plus 2 tablespoons all-purpose flour, unsifted
1 teaspoon baking powder
1/2 teaspoon baking soda
1/2 teaspoon salt
1 6-ounce package semi-sweet chocolate morsels
1 cup raisins
1/2 cup nuts, finely chopped

Combine shortening, sugar, and eggs; beat until creamy. In a small bowl combine milk, vinegar and banana. In another bowl combine flour, baking powder, soda, and salt. Stir these mixtures into creamed mixture alternately. Fold in chocolate morsels, raisins, and nuts. Pour into four well greased and floured 6 x 3½ x 2-inch loaf pans or one 9 x 5 x 3-inch loaf pan. Bake at 375 degrees for 25-30 minutes. Remove from pans immediately.

Mrs. Joe Woodard (Jerry)
Similar recipes submitted by:
Mrs. Robert Mullins (JoAnn),
Mrs. Carroll Sullivan Mobile, Alabama

PUMPKIN BREAD

"Ideal for a neighbor's Christmas treat."

3½ cups plain flour, sifted
2 teaspoons soda
1½ teaspoons salt
1 teaspoon nutmeg
1½ teaspoons cinnamon
3 cups sugar
1 cup cooking oil
4 eggs
2/3 cup cold tap water
1 16-ounce can pumpkin
1 cup pecans, chopped

Measure and sift dry ingredients into large mixing bowl. Add cooking oil. Add eggs one at a time; mix well with mixer on medium speed. Add water and pumpkin and continue to mix until smooth. Stir nuts into mixture. Pour into well greased and floured 9 x 5 x 3-inch loaf pans or 1 bundt pan. Bake at 350 degrees about 1 hour or until toothpick comes out clean. Great toasted with butter. Preparation time 30 minutes. Makes 2 loaves.

Mrs. Stanley Thornton (Cathy)
Mrs. Andy Lowery Huntsville, Alabama

ALL-PURPOSE CREPE BATTER

4 eggs
¼ teaspoon salt
2 cups plain flour
2¼ cups milk
¼ cup butter, melted

Mixer or Whisk method:
In medium bowl, combine eggs and salt. Gradually add flour alternating with milk, beating with electric mixer or whisk until smooth. Beat in melted butter. Refrigerate for at least 1 hour before using.

Blender method:
Combine ingredients in blender container; blend about 1 minute. Scrape down sides with rubber spatula and blend for another 15 seconds or until smooth. Refrigerate for at least 1 hour before using.
Makes about 32 crepes.
Mrs. Jay Thornton (Willene,

FAVORITE PANCAKES

"Light as a feather."

1¼ cups all-purpose flour, sifted
2 teaspoons baking powder
½ teaspoon soda
1 tablespoon sugar
½ teaspoon salt
1 egg, beaten
1 cup buttermilk
2 tablespoons salad oil

Sift together dry ingredients. Combine egg, buttermilk, and oil. Add to dry ingredients, stirring until flour is moistened (batter will be lumpy). Bake on a hot griddle. This can be made in a blender. For a variation 1 cup blueberries may be added. Makes 12 dollar-size pancakes or 8 4-inch ones.
Mrs. Larry Barksdale (Fran)

BEER BREAD

"Quick, easy, and so delicious."

3 cups self-rising flour
1 teaspoon salt
3 tablespoons sugar
1 12-ounce can beer

Mix all ingredients. Pour into greased 9 x 5 x 3-inch loaf pan. Bake 1 hour in 350 degree oven.
Mrs. Tom Bailey *Little Rock, Arkansas*

FRENCH BREAD

½ cup milk
¾ cup boiling water
2 teaspoons yeast
½ cup warm water
1½ tablespoons butter, melted
1 tablespoon sugar
4 cups all-purpose flour
2 teaspoons salt
2 teaspoons sugar
1 egg white, beaten
1 tablespoon cold water

Scald ½ cup milk and add ¾ cup boiling water. While liquid cools dissolve yeast in ½ cup warm water. Let yeast rest for 10 minutes then add it to the milk mixture; next add melted butter and 1 tablespoon sugar. In a large mixing bowl place flour, 2 teaspoons salt and 2 teaspoons sugar and then sift together. Make a hole in the center of these ingredients and pour in liquid mixture. Stir completely, but do not knead. Cover with a damp cloth and put in an unheated oven on the top shelf. Put a pan of boiling water on the bottom shelf and allow dough to rise 2 hours. Punch down dough. On a floured board pat into two equal oblongs. Form a loaf by rolling oblong toward you. Continue rolling and pressing the dough toward the ends until a long, thin form is made. Place loaves on a well greased cookie sheet cutting ¼ inch slit in the top with a sharp knife. Set in a warm place and allow to rise to about double. Preheat oven to 400 degrees. In the bottom of the oven, place a pan with ½ inch boiling water. Bake for 15 minutes; then reduce heat to 350 degrees and bake 30 minutes longer. Five minutes before bread is done brush loaves with a mixture of 1 beaten egg white and 1 tablespoon water.
Mr. William B. McGehee, III

SPOON BREAD

"Great, when left over, with creamed chicken or ham."

1 cup hot water
1 cup cornmeal
2 tablespoons shortening
1 teaspoon salt
1 tablespoon sugar
½ teaspoon soda
1 cup buttermilk
2 eggs, beaten

Mix water and cornmeal together. Add shortening, salt, and sugar. Dissolve soda in buttermilk and add to cornmeal mixture. Add eggs and mix well. Pour into well greased baking dish. Bake 30 to 40 minutes at 375 degrees. Spoon hot from pan. Delicious with a vegetable meal.
Mrs. Guy Kaylor (Florence)
Similar recipes submitted by Mrs. John Graves (Evalina), Mrs. Joe L. Wallis (Dot)

JALAPENO CORNBREAD

"For that South of the Border flavor."

1 cup yellow cornmeal
1 cup buttermilk
2 eggs
¼ to ½ cup bacon drippings
¾ teaspoon soda
½ teaspoon salt
1 large onion, chopped
½ to 1 Jalapeno pepper, chopped
½ cup cream-style corn
½ pound Cheddar cheese, grated

Mix all ingredients except cheese. Pour half of mixture into large iron skillet. Cover with cheese. Pour on remaining batter. Bake at 400 degrees until brown. Lower heat to 375 degrees and bake 10 minutes longer. Serves 8-10.

Mrs. Michael Reeves (Susan)

SUNSET BREAD OR ROLLS

1 cup milk
½ cup sugar
1 teaspoon salt
½ cup margarine or butter
1 package yeast
¼ cup warm water
3 eggs, slightly beaten
4¾ cups all-purpose flour or (up to 2¾ cups wholewheat flour can be used instead of all-purpose flour)

Scald milk and pour over sugar, salt and butter in large bowl. Cool to lukewarm. Soften yeast in warm water. Add to mixture along with the eggs. Gradually stir in flour to make a soft dough. Cover and let rise in a warm place until it puffs up, (approximately 30 minutes). Punch down. Cover with plastic wrap and refrigerate for 2-3 hours. Punch down and knead lightly on a lightly floured board for 1 minute. Cover and refrigerate for 4 hours or overnight. Shape dough and put in a greased 5 x 9-inch loaf pan, (4 pans). Let the dough rise until double. Bake at 350 degrees for 45 minutes for the bread. For rolls bake at 350 degrees for 25 minutes.

Mrs. Michael H. Cleckler (Karen)

HEAVENLY BREAD

"Winter's best snack – bread warm from the oven."

1 14-ounce can Eagle Brand milk add enough water to make 2 cups
2 cups water
1 teaspoon salt
1 stick margarine
2 packages dry yeast
½ cup tepid water
12 cups flour, sifted

Combine liquids, salt, and margarine in saucepan. Heat to melt margarine. Pour liquids into large bowl and cool. Dissolve yeast in tepid water; add to cooled mixture and let rise until puffy. Beat in seven cups flour. Let rise one to two hours. Add five cups flour and mix well (use rolling pin and beat to make smooth). Divide into four parts; place in well greased 9 x 5 x 3-inch loaf pans and let rise one hour. Bake 25-30 minutes at 350 degrees. Makes 4 loaves.
Mrs. Myron Waits (Miller)

GERMAN CORNBREAD

"Great with chili or homemade vegetable soup."

1½ cups self-rising cornmeal
2 eggs
½ cup Wesson oil
1 8-ounce can cream-style corn
1 cup sour cream
1 large onion, chopped

Mix all ingredients together. Pour into a greased skillet. Bake 30-35 minutes or until brown at 400 degrees.
Mrs. Robert Burgess (Eloise)

CHEESE BREAD BISCUITS

1 5-ounce jar Old English cheese
1 stick margarine
½ teaspoon red pepper
1 egg, beaten
1 loaf sandwich bread

Let cheese and margarine soften at room temperature. Blend thoroughly all ingredients except bread. Trim crusts from bread and cut each slice into four squares. Spread cheese mixture between two squares and ice top and sides. Bake at 350 degrees for 10-15 minutes. Serve hot with coffee, brunch, or at mealtime.
Mrs. Ramond C. Hammett (Louise)

MEXICAN CORNBREAD

"Add a tossed salad – your meal is ready."

1 16-ounce can cream-style corn
1 cup self-rising cornmeal
2 eggs
1 4-ounce can green chili peppers, chopped
1 to 2 Jalapeno peppers, chopped
1 pound ground beef
2 small onions, chopped
1 teaspoon salt
½ teaspoon pepper
½ teaspoon garlic salt
1½ cups cheese, grated

Mix corn, cornmeal, and eggs. Add peppers. Pour one half mixture into 12-inch iron skillet. Combine beef, onions, and seasonings in another skillet and brown. Pour one half over cornmeal mixture and sprinkle with cheese. Add remaining cornmeal mixture; then meat. Bake 50-60 minutes at 350 degrees.
Mrs. Joe Woodard (Jerry)

EASY ICE-BOX ROLLS

"Great to have on hand."

¾ cup margarine, melted
1 package dry yeast
4 cups self-rising flour
¼ cup sugar
1 egg, slightly beaten
2 cups warm water

Melt margarine and cool to lukewarm. In large mixing bowl combine yeast and flour. Add other ingredients and stir until blended. Dough will be soft and sticky. Put in airtight container and store in refrigerator several hours. Spoon by teaspoonsful into muffin cups. Bake at 400 degrees for 20 minutes. Keeps in refrigerator for one week. Small rolls are better.
Mrs. David Beasley (Ellen)

AUNT JULE'S NEVER FAIL REFRIGERATOR ROLLS

"A family favorite for generations."

1 yeast cake or 1 package yeast
1 tablespoon sugar
1 cup warm water
3 medium potatoes
⅔ cup sugar
2 eggs, beaten
1 cup milk, scalded
5 cups plain flour, sifted
1 teaspoon salt
½ cup shortening

Dissolve yeast and sugar in water for one half hour. Boil potatoes; mash and use 1½ cups. Add sugar and eggs; mix well. In saucepan, scald milk. Add to potato mixture, stirring until smooth. Add yeast and mix well. Cover and let rise one hour. Sift flour. Add flour, salt, and shortening; knead about 5 minutes. Add more flour, if needed, to make dough soft. Place in greased bowl; cover and refrigerate at least 3-4 hours or over night. Shape rolls as needed; let rise 1½ hours in warm place. Bake at 425 degrees for 15 minutes. These will keep 3-4 days in the refrigerator.
Mrs. William Lawrence (Sally)

FREEZER BISCUITS

"If you like to think ahead, try this."

5 cups flour, sifted
¼ cup sugar
3 teaspoons baking powder
1 teaspoon soda
1 teaspoon salt
1 cup shortening
1 package dry yeast
2 tablespoons warm water
2 cups buttermilk

Sift dry ingredients together. Cut in shortening. Dissolve yeast in warm water and add to buttermilk. Add mixture to dry ingredients and mix well. Turn out on lightly floured board. Roll out and cut. Place on cookie sheet and freeze. After frozen, store in freezer bags. About 30 minutes before baking take out and brush with melted butter. Bake at 350 degrees until brown.
Mrs. Robert Mullins (JoAnn)

WHOLE WHEAT ROLLS OR LOAVES

"A bread for spreads – try it with butter, jelly, jam."

½ cup shortening
½ cup sugar
2 cups boiling water
1 package dry yeast
⅓ cup lukewarm water
4 cups whole wheat flour
2 scant cups white flour
1 teaspoon salt
2 tablespoons shortening

In 2-quart saucepan, dissolve shortening and sugar in boiling water and cool to lukewarm. Prepare yeast in lukewarm water. Sift flours and salt into saucepan. Add yeast mixture and beat with spoon. Dough should be soft and sticky. Place in refrigerator for 8 hours or overnight. Knead thoroughly, adding as little of either flour as possible to make dough manageable. To make rolls, roll dough ½ inch thick and cut with 2-inch cutter. Melt shortening; coat rolls; fold in half and place on greased cookie sheet. Bake at 400 degrees for 15 minutes. To make loaves divide dough in half and form loaf; coat in shortening and place in greased 9 x 5 x 3-inch loaf pans. Let rise 2 hours. Bake 350 degrees for 45-60 minutes. Dough may be frozen uncooked or kept in refrigerator for one week. Makes 2 loaves or 48 rolls.

Mrs. J. H. Johnson (Eleanor)

BISCUITS SUPREME

"A real compliment getter – yet so easy to make."

2 cups all-purpose flour, sifted
4 teaspoons baking powder
½ teaspoon salt
½ teaspoon cream of tartar
2 teaspoons sugar
½ cup shortening
⅔ cup milk

Sift together dry ingredients. Cut in shortening till mixture resembles coarse crumbs. Add milk and stir. Turn out on a lightly floured surface; knead gently ½ minute. Pat or roll ½ inch thick. Cut with biscuit cutter. Bake on greased cookie sheet at 450 degrees for 10-12 minutes. Makes 16 biscuits.

Mrs. William B. McGehee, III (Evelyn)
Mrs. Larry Barksdale (Fran)

BEER BISCUITS

"Bet you can't eat just one of these."

4 cups Bisquick
2 tablespoons sugar
1 12-ounce can beer

Combine all ingredients. Pour into greased muffin tins. Fill one half full. Bake at 425 degrees until brown. Makes 2 dozen.
Mrs. Charles Nelson (Mary)
Mrs. Larkin Coker (Joan)

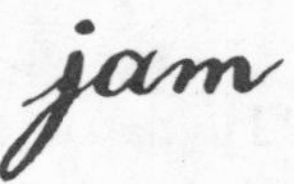

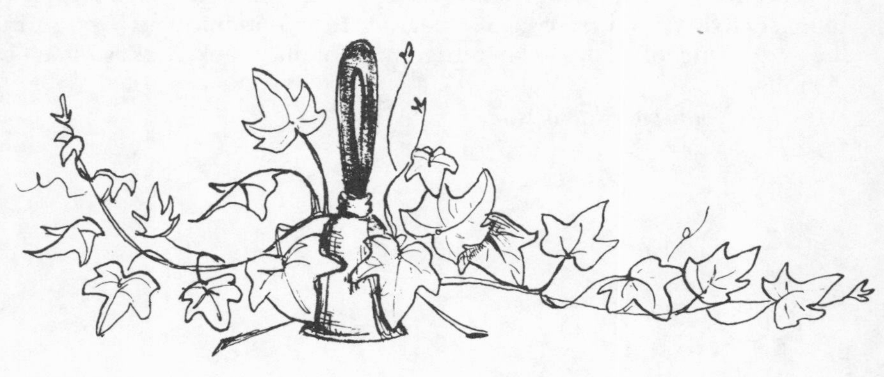

SUNSET JAM

"Simple to make, good to eat."

2 pounds pears (22 medium or 7 cups, grated)
1 cup crushed pineapple
1 cup cherries, halved
5 cups sugar
Juice one lemon
1 box Sure Jell

Wash, peel, and grate pears. In large saucepan place all ingredients except Sure Jell and cook over medium heat. Bring to boil and continue to cook for 6 minutes. Stir occasionally. Add Sure Jell and boil one minute. Pour into hot sterilized jars and seal.
Mrs. Ralph Gaines, Jr., (Mary Sue)

FIG JAM

"Like sunshine on a breakfast table."

2 quarts (about 5 pounds) fresh figs, chopped
¾ cup water
6 cups sugar
¼ cup lemon juice

Pour boiling water over figs and let stand 10 minutes. Drain, stem, and chop figs (a blender may be used). Add water and sugar to figs and place in large saucepan. Slowly bring to boil, stirring occasionally until sugar dissolves. Cook rapidly until thick, stirring frequently to prevent sticking. Add lemon juice and cook one minute longer. Pour boiling hot into sterilized jars. Adjust self-sealing caps. Makes 5-6 pints.
Mrs. Jack Clark (Becky)

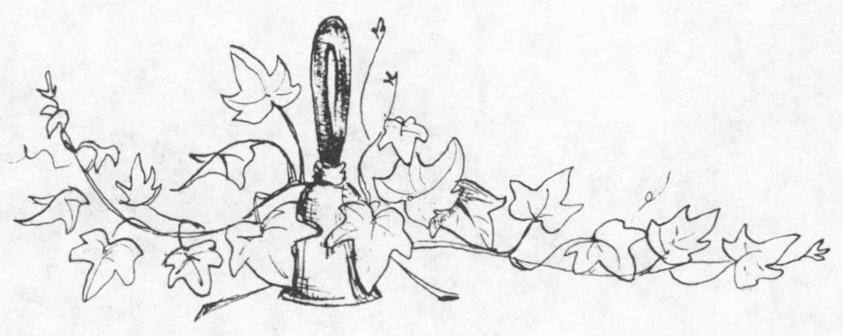

L & N Depot
by Louise Abernethy

Entrees

cheese and eggs

CURRIED EGGS IN SHRIMP SAUCE

8 hard-boiled eggs
⅓ cup mayonnaise
¼ teaspoon mustard
½ teaspoon salt
½ teaspoon curry powder
½ teaspoon paprika

Cut eggs lengthwise. Remove yolks. Mash yolks and mix with remaining ingredients. Fill cavities with mixture. Arrange eggs in greased glass baking dish.

Sauce:

2 tablespoons butter
2 tablespoons flour
1½ cups milk
½ cup American cheese, shredded
1 can shrimp soup
1 cup bread crumbs, toasted and buttered
2 tablespoons butter

Blend 2 tablespoons butter and flour in sauce pan. Add milk and stir constantly over low heat. Add soup and cheese, stir until thick and smooth. Pour over eggs. Sprinkle with bread crumbs and dot with 2 tablespoons butter. Bake in oven at 350 degrees for 25-30 minutes. Serves 6-8.
Mrs. Frank Harwell (Edith)

QUICHE LORRAINE

½ pound bacon
1 9 inch deep dish pie shell, unbaked
1½ cups Swiss cheese, grated
1 tablespoon bacon fat
1 medium onion, minced
3 eggs
1 cup heavy cream
½ cup milk
½ teaspoon salt
¼ teaspoon pepper
Dash cayenne pepper
½ teaspoon dry mustard
1 cup fresh mushrooms, sliced

Cook 1 slice bacon until limp. Cut in 1 inch pieces and set aside. Cook remaining bacon until crisp. Drain and crumble into pie shell. Sprinkle cheese over bacon. Sauté onion in 1 tablespoon bacon fat until golden brown. Drain and sprinkle over cheese. Sauté mushrooms in butter. When ready to bake, combine eggs, cream, milk, seasoning, and mushrooms. Pour into pie shell. Decorate with bacon pieces and a few strips of cheese. Bake in pre-heated oven at 375 degrees. Serves 10-12 as an appetizer or 6 for dinner.
Mrs. Mike Reeves (Susan)
Similar recipes submitted by:
Mrs. Henry Rush (Selena)
Mrs. Danny Harris (Joan)

MEXICAN QUICHE

"A marvelous blend of France and Mexico."

½ pint whole sweet cream
3 eggs, well beaten
¼ teaspoon salt
⅛ teaspoon cumin
1½ cups Monterey Jack cheese, shredded
1 cup Cheddar cheese, shredded
3 El Paso pickled hot Jalapenos, chopped
3 unbaked frozen pie crusts

Mix together cream, eggs, salt, and cumin. Sprinkle all of Monterey Jack and ½ of Cheddar over bottoms of pie crusts. Then sprinkle hot peppers and the remainder of Cheddar over mixture. Pour the sweet cream mixture over layered cheese and peppers. Bake in 350 degree oven 45-50 minutes or until mixture and crusts are done. Do not over bake or pies will be dry.
Mrs. John Barksdale (Dorothy)

MACARONI AND CHEESE

"Easy and Tasty."

1 cup macaroni
1 cup cottage cheese
1 cup sharp Cheddar cheese,, grated
1 egg, beaten
½ cup sour cream

Cook macaroni and drain. Mix with cheeses, egg, and sour cream. Bake at 350 degrees for 30-40 minutes in 2 quart casserole.
Mrs. Randy Beard Guntersville, Alabama

SPICY EGG CASSEROLE

2 10-ounce cans Rotel tomatoes, drained
1 pound sharp cheese, grated
4 eggs, beaten
3 cups milk
1 cup flour
2 teaspoons salt
1 teaspoon mustard
2 tablespoons Worcestershire sauce
1 teaspoon sweet basil
¼ green pepper, chopped
¼ cup green onions, chopped
Sprinkle of paprika
¼ cup Bacos

Add all ingredients together and pour in greased casserole. Bake at 350 degrees for 1 hour. Serves 10.
Mrs. Tom Bailey Little Rock, Arkansas

EGGS SUPREME

"A St. Louis Symphony Cookbook Recipe."

2 tablespoons butter
2 tablespoons flour
1 cup milk
½ cup cream
½ teaspoon Worcestershire sauce
8 hard-cooked eggs
1 cup ham, diced
1 teaspoon salt
⅛ teaspoon paprika
1 cup cooked rice
½ cup Cheddar cheese, grated

Melt butter and blend in flour. Remove from heat and gradually stir in milk. Stir over low heat until it boils 1 minute. Remove from heat and stir in rest of ingredients except rice and cheese. Pour into greased 8-inch Pyrex dish. Sprinkle rice and cheese over top. Bake at 350 degrees for 45 minutes. Serves 6-8.

Mrs. Tom Bailey Little Rock, Arkansas
Similar recipe submitted by Mrs. Pope Wilder (Frances)

MACARONI CASSEROLE

"Don't pass this by."

1 pound sharp cheese, grated
1 cup macaroni, uncooked
1 can cream of mushroom soup
1 cup mayonnaise
1 onion, grated
1 small jar chopped pimiento

Cook macaroni in salt water. Drain. Mix macaroni and remaining ingredients in greased 1½-quart casserole. Bake in preheated 375 degree oven for 45 minutes.

Mrs. Norman Wood (Madge)

BREAKFAST PIE

3 eggs
1 cup sharp Cheddar cheese, grated
½ of 13-ounce can Pet milk
Salt and pepper to taste
1 9 inch pie shell, thawed

Place all ingredients in blender. When mixed, pour in unbaked pie shell and bake for 30 minutes at 350 degrees.

Mrs. Toby Deese (Ruth Helen)

CHEESE STRATA

*"A wonderful idea for Brunch.
Add some chopped ham, if you wish."*

6 slices light bread
3 eggs, well beaten
2 cups sweet milk
1 teaspoon salt
1 teaspoon dry mustard
1 teaspoon baking powder
Dash of red pepper
2 cups aged Wisconsin cheese, grated

Break up bread in 2 quart greased casserole. Sprinkle 1 layer of cheese in bottom of dish. Mix eggs, milk, salt, mustard, baking powder, and pepper. Pour over bread and cheese and refrigerate at least 1 hour or overnight. Bake at 350 degrees for 45 minutes. This is better if made ahead. The bread absorbs liquid and gives it a lighter texture. Serves 6.

Mrs. Winston Legge (Sarah)
Similar recipes submitted by:
Mrs. William Lawrence (Sally)
Mrs. Bob Chapman (Mildred)
Mrs. Raymond Hammett (Louise)

CHEESE ENCHILADAS

2 medium onions, chopped
2 large green peppers, chopped
3 tablespoons salad oil
2 10-ounce cans enchilada sauce
1 cup sour cream
12 corn tortillas
¼ cup salad oil
1 pound Monterey Jack cheese, cut in slices
2 cups mild Cheddar cheese, shredded

Cook onion and green peppers in 3 tablespoons salad oil until soft. Salt to taste and set aside. Combine enchilada sauce and sour cream. Simmer 1 minute. Fry tortillas one at a time in salad oil for a few seconds on each side. Do not overcook. Drain on paper towel. Put a thin coating of enchilada sauce in bottom of large baking dish. Layer onion and pepper mixture on tortillas and then Monterey Jack cheese. Roll tortillas and place in baking dish, seam side down. Pour remaining sauce over tortillas and top with Cheddar cheese. Bake uncovered at 375 degrees for 20-30 minutes. Serves 4.

Mrs. Otis R. Burton (Louise)

chicken

CHICKEN SAUTÉ, MASCOTTE

4 chicken breasts, split
Salt, pepper and paprika to taste
2 tablespoons butter
2 tablespoons oil
1/8 teaspoon crumbled dried tarragon
1/8 teaspoon crumbled dried rosemary
1/2 pound fresh mushrooms
Juice of 1 lemon
3/4 cup dry white wine
2 tablespoons sherry
2 teaspoons chicken stock base
1 11-ounce can artichoke hearts
Finely chopped parsley for garnish

Season chicken pieces with salt, pepper, and paprika. Using a large frying pan, brown chicken in butter and oil. Sprinkle with tarragon and rosemary. Cover and cook over medium heat for 20 to 25 minutes or until tender. Remove chicken to a platter and keep warm. Quarter mushrooms and add to pan with lemon juice, white wine, sherry, and stock base; let cook a few minutes. Add artichokes to the pan juices and heat until hot through. Spoon vegetables from sauce over chicken pieces. Quickly cook down sauce in pan until smooth and thick; spoon over all and sprinkle with parsley. Serves 8.

Mrs. Carson Whitson (Sarah)

CHICKEN-ALMOND QUICHE

1 9-inch unbaked pie shell
1 cup chicken, cooked and diced
3 tablespoons slivered almonds
1½ cups Swiss cheese, shredded
3 eggs, slightly beaten
1½ cups milk
½ teaspoon salt
¼ teaspoon mace
⅛ teaspoon pepper
2 tablespoons Parmesan cheese

Place chicken and almonds in pie shell. Sprinkle Swiss cheese over both. In a separate bowl combine the eggs, milk, salt, mace and pepper. Pour over cheese, chicken and almonds. Sprinkle with Parmesan cheese. Bake at 375 degrees for 30-35 minutes, or until knife comes out clean. Allow to stand 10 minutes before serving. Freezes well. Serves 6.
Mrs. Wallace Twiggs (Linda S.)

CHICKEN ADELE

"A best-ever way to fix chicken."

4 cups chicken, cut up
1 medium onion, chopped
3 stalks celery, chopped
2 cups bread crumbs
2 cups chicken broth
4 eggs
1 cup New York sharp cheese, grated
½ cup mayonnaise
Salt and pepper to taste
1 box cornflakes (medium)
Slivered almonds

Boil chicken in water with onion and celery. Drain and cube. (Reserve 2 cups of chicken broth). Mix chicken, bread crumbs, chicken broth, eggs, cheese, mayonnaise, salt and pepper to taste. Pour into a greased square or oblong casserole. Refrigerate over night. When ready to use, let come to room temperature. Crush cornflakes and put on top, then a layer of slivered almonds, ending with a layer of cornflakes. Dot with margarine. Place in pan of hot water and bake approximately 45 minutes at 325 degrees. Cover with foil for first 30 minutes, remove and finish cooking. Cut into squares and serve with mushroom sauce.

Mushroom Sauce:

1 can mushroom soup
½ can water
1 small can mushroom pieces, drained
Margarine

Simmer mushroom pieces in margarine approximately 5 minutes. Add soup and water. Cook until hot.
Mrs. Charles H. Miller (Floyce)

CHICKEN LIVERS SUPREME

"Serve over toast points for a luncheon dish."

8 slices bacon
6 green onions, including tops
2 pounds chicken livers
2 tablespoons butter
Salt and pepper to taste
2 dashes Tabasco
2 tablespoons Worcestershire sauce
1 can cream of mushroom soup
Parsley or paprika (optional)

Fry bacon until crisp. Set aside. Dice green onions and cook in bacon fat 5 minutes. Set aside. Place chicken livers in bacon fat and add butter. Cook over medium heat turning frequently just until pink disappears — approximately 10 to 12 minutes. Add salt and pepper to taste. Combine Tabasco and Worcestershire with mushroom soup, mixing well. Remove chicken livers to a 1½-quart chafing dish; add sautéed green onions. Lightly stir in soup mixture; crumble bacon over top. A garnish of chopped parsley or paprika may be added for color. Serve over toast points. Serves 8.

Mrs. Stratton Lawrence (Elsie)

CHICKEN CREPES WITH CHEESE SAUCE

¼ cup butter
¼ cup flour
2 cups chicken broth
2 teaspoons Worcestershire sauce
3 cups Cheddar cheese, grated
2 cups sour cream
2 10-ounce packages broccoli spears, cooked
2 cups chicken, cooked and chopped
12 crepes, cooked

Over medium heat melt butter in small saucepan. Stir in flour and cook until bubbly. Add broth and Worcestershire sauce; cook, stirring until thickened. Add 2 cups cheese. Empty sour cream into medium bowl; gradually add hot cheese sauce, stirring constantly. In large shallow baking dish, place cooked broccoli and chicken on each crepe. Spoon 1 tablespoon sauce over each. Fold crepes over. Pour remaining sauce over all. Sprinkle with remaining cheese. Cover. Bake 350 degrees for 20 to 30 minutes. Serves 12.

Mrs. Jay Thornton (Willene)

CHICKEN DIVAN

"Always a favorite."

2 cups chicken, cooked and sliced
2 cans cream of chicken soup
2 boxes frozen broccoli spears, cooked and drained
1 cup mayonnaise
1 cup cheese, grated
1 teaspoon curry powder
1 cup buttered bread crumbs

Place broccoli in 9 x 13-inch buttered baking dish; cover with cooked chicken. Mix mayonnaise, soup and curry powder and pour over chicken. Sprinkle cheese and bread crumbs over this mixture. Bake at 350 degrees until bubbly, approximately 30 minutes.
Mrs. Tommy Barber (Betty)

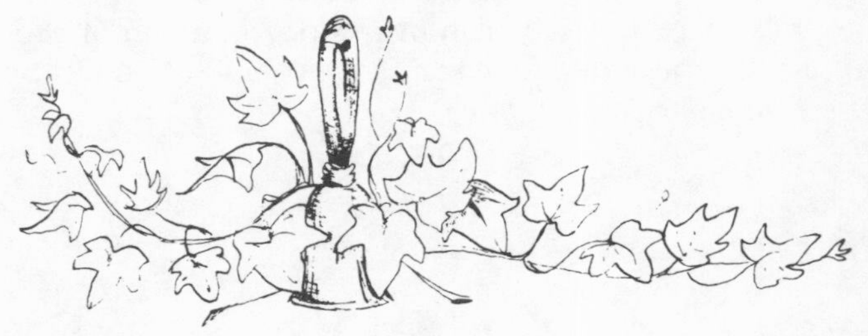

CLASSIC CHICKEN DIVAN

"A dish that is a meal in itself."

2 bunches fresh broccoli or 2 10-ounce packages frozen broccoli
¼ cup butter or margarine
¼ cup flour
2 cups chicken broth
½ cup light cream
3 tablespoons sherry wine
½ teaspoon salt
Dash of pepper
3 whole chicken breasts, cooked, boned and thinly sliced
¼ cup Parmesan cheese

Cook broccoli in boiling salted water; drain. Melt butter, blend in flour. Add chicken broth, stirring until thick. Stir in cream, sherry, salt and pepper. Place broccoli cross-wise in 13 x 9 x 2-inch baking dish. Pour one-half the sauce over broccoli, top with chicken slices. Add Parmesan cheese to remaining sauce; pour over chicken. Sprinkle with additional Parmesan cheese. Bake at 350 degrees for 20 minutes or until heated through. Broil until sauce is golden. Can be frozen in freezer-to-oven type baking dish. It can also be made and stored in refrigerator the day before it is to be baked. Serves 8.
Mrs. James Naff (Irene)

CHICKEN AND DRIED BEEF

"A combination of chicken, beef and bacon that is superb."

4 to 6 chicken breasts, boned
3 slices bacon
1 jar Armour Dried Beef
½ pint sour cream
1 can mushroom soup

Wrap each chicken breast with ½ slice of bacon. Put on bed of dried beef (cut-up). Mix sour cream and soup. Spoon over chicken. Bake at 250 degrees uncovered for 4-4½ hours. Serves 4.
Mrs. James D. Luker, Jr. (Judy)

CHICKEN BISCUIT DUMPLINGS

"The whole family will enjoy this."

1 can cream of chicken soup
1¼ cups water
½ cup green pepper, chopped
2 tablespoons onion, chopped

In a 3 quart saucepan, combine all ingredients. Heat, stirring occasionally until bubbly.

Dumplings:

1½ cups chicken, cooked and cubed
¼ cup celery, chopped
2 tablespoons onion, chopped
1 teaspoon parsley flakes
⅛ to ¼ teaspoon pepper
1 8-ounce can buttermilk biscuits

Combine all ingredients in mixing bowl except biscuits; mix well. Separate biscuit dough into 10 biscuits, pat or roll out each to about 4-inch circle. Place ¼ cup chicken mixture on each circle; wrap dough around mixture firmly pressing edges to seal. Place sealed edge of biscuit down into bubbling soup mixture. Spoon soup over dumplings. Cover tightly and cook over medium heat 15-20 minutes until dumplings are no longer doughy. Serve hot with soup mixture. Dumplings can be made ahead, covered and refrigerated up to 2 hours before cooking. Entree may be covered and reheated over medium heat 15-20 minutes if prepared ahead or as a left over.
Mrs. James F. Camp (Gayle)
Similar recipe submitted by Mrs. Pat Duke (Carolyn)

CHICKEN WITH ARTICHOKES

1 2-pound chicken
1 bell pepper, chopped
1 onion, sliced thin
½ cup olive oil
¼ cup butter
½ pound fresh mushrooms, sliced
1 box wild rice
1 14-ounce can artichoke hearts, drained
Toasted almonds

Boil chicken until done. Debone and cut into chunks. While chicken is boiling, sauté chopped bell pepper and onion in olive oil. In another pan sauté fresh mushrooms in butter. Cook wild rice according to package directions. Fold all together and place in greased 2-quart casserole. Tear apart artichoke hearts and arrange in casserole. Bake at 350 degrees for 35 minutes. Sprinkle almonds over top and bake 5 minutes longer. Serves 6.
Mrs. W. B. McGehee, III (Evelyn)

CHILI CHICKEN BAKE

1 average size fryer (cut for frying)
1 cup chili sauce
¼ cup chopped onions
1 tablespoon vinegar

Brown chicken in butter. Mix chili sauce, onions, and vinegar. Pour mixture over chicken. Cover tightly. Bake at 350 degrees for 1-1½ hours.
Mrs. Desoto Burton (Wells)

CHICKEN BREASTS SUPREME

3 *whole* chicken breasts, cut in half lengthwise
¾ teaspoon seasoned salt
Dash of paprika (to taste)
1 chicken bouillon cube
1 cup boiling water
¼ cup sauterne or chablis
1½ teaspoon finely chopped onion
½ teaspoon curry powder
Dash of pepper

Sprinkle chicken with salt and paprika and place in 9 x 13-inch casserole. Dissolve bouillon in boiling water; add wine, onion, curry powder and pepper. Pour over chicken. Cover with foil; bake at 350 degrees for 30 minutes. Uncover and bake 30-45 minutes longer. Serves 6.
Mrs. Dean Parker Mobile, Alabama

CHICKEN HOW-SO

"This is a sumptuous way to fix chicken."

4 chicken breasts, skinned and boned
2 tablespoons butter
1 can golden mushroom soup
½ cup water
1 beef bouillon cube
1 tablespoon soy sauce
1 teaspoon Worcestershire
½ teaspoon curry powder
½ teaspoon poppy seed
1 8-ounce can bamboo shoots, drained
½ cup celery, sliced
½ cup onion, sliced
1 3-ounce can mushrooms, sliced and drained
1 small green pepper, cut in strips
3 tablespoons white wine
1 3-ounce can chow mein noodles

Cut chicken into 1½-inch pieces. In skillet, brown chicken in butter until golden brown. Stir in the soup, water, bouillon, soy sauce, Worcestershire, curry powder and poppy seed; mix well. Cover and simmer 15 minutes. Stir occasionally. Add bamboo shoots, celery, onion and mushrooms. Cover and simmer 10 minutes or until tender and crisp. Stir in green pepper and wine; cover and simmer 2-3 minutes. Serve over rice and top with chow mein noodles.

Mrs. Dennis Ronning *Savannah, Georgia*

CHICKEN-RICE DISH

1 large fryer
1 10½-ounce can cream of chicken soup
¾ cup mayonnaise
1 cup rice, cooked
1 teaspoon onion, grated
1 cup celery, chopped
1 teaspoon lemon juice
½ teaspoon salt
2 tablespoons Worcestershire
3 boiled eggs
½ cup slivered almonds
Potato chips

Cook and cube chicken. Mix soup, mayonnaise, celery, rice, onion, lemon juice, salt, Worcestershire and almonds. Add chicken and eggs. Bake in 9 x 13-inch baking dish. Cover with potato chips. Bake at 375 degrees for 25 minutes. This can be made ahead and frozen. Leave potato chips off when freezing. Serves 8.

Mrs. James B. White, Jr. (Evelyn B.)

GINGER CHICKEN

"Good with green beans and a strawberry congealed salad."

¼ pound butter
1 bunch scallions (or 2 green onions) chopped in 1 inch pieces
1 teaspoon powdered ginger or 1 tablespoon fresh grated ginger
1 can water chestnuts drained and sliced
2 cups chopped cooked chicken in 2 inch pieces
1 4-ounce can mushroom caps
½ teaspoon salt
½ teaspoon pepper
4 tablespoons sour cream

Mix all ingredients, except sour cream. Heat thoroughly. Stir in sour cream. Serve immediately over rice with tablespoons of sour cream topping each serving. Serves 4-6.
Mrs. Joe Woodard (Jerry)

BAKED CHICKEN SANDWICHES

1½ cups chicken, cooked and diced
1 can mushroom soup, undiluted
1 tablespoon minced onions
1 2-ounce jar pimiento, chopped
3 tablespoons flour
¾ cup milk
12 slices bread
3 tablespoons milk
2 eggs
Potato chips
Slivered almonds

Combine first four ingredients. Blend 3 tablespoons flour in ¾ cup milk. Cook to thicken; cool and chill. Remove crusts from bread. Put 6 slices of bread in an oblong pyrex dish. Cover with chicken mixture and the remaining bread. Saran wrap and chill over night. Mix 3 tablespoons milk into 2 fork beaten eggs. Cut sandwiches in half; dip in batter, then crushed potato chips; put on buttered cookie sheet — not touching; sprinkle with slivered almonds and bake at 350 degrees for 20 to 25 minutes. Serves 6.
Mrs. A. F. Toole (Barbara)

CHICKEN TETRAZZINI I

"This recipe attributed to Luisa Tetrazzini, famous operatic soprano."

½ pound spaghetti
2 cups mushrooms, sliced
4 cups Velonté sauce
2 to 3 cups chicken, cooked
4 tablespoons oleo
⅔ cup Parmesan cheese
½ cup slivered almonds, toasted

Velonté Sauce:

4 tablespoons butter
2 cups chicken stock
½ cup flour
⅔ cup cream
¼ cup sherry
Salt and pepper
Dash of Nutmeg, optional

Break spaghetti into one inch pieces. Cook and drain. Sauté mushrooms in butter. Make sauce in double boiler, cook until thickened. Season with sherry and a dash of nutmeg, if desired. Layer spaghetti, chicken and mushrooms, pouring sauce on each layer. Sprinkle with almonds, then cheese. Bake at 400 degrees until bubbly and browned. Serves 8.
Mrs. Allen Jacobs (Hope)

CHICKEN TETRAZZINI II

½ stick margarine
¼ cup flour
2 cups chicken broth
¼ teaspoon turmeric
½ teaspoon Accent
1 teaspoon salt
⅛ teaspoon pepper
1 cup heavy cream
2 to 3 cups diced chicken (cooked)
1 small can mushrooms, drained
¼ cup slivered almonds, toasted
¼ cup Parmesan cheese
¼ cup American cheese, grated
2 to 3 pimientoes, cut up
Paprika (for top)
12-ounce package of spaghetti or vermicelli

Cook spaghetti or vermicelli while making sauce. Make sauce of first three ingredients in double boiler. Remove from heat and stir in seasonings and cream. Combine half the sauce with well drained spaghetti or vermicelli and place in shallow casserole. Combine remaining sauce with chicken, mushrooms, almonds and pimientoes. Place in center of casserole and sprinkle with cheeses and paprika. Bake at 375 degrees approximately 30 minutes or until lightly browned. Serves 10-12.
Mrs. Alec O. Thomson (Catherine C.)

CHICKEN TETRAZZINI III

"Excellent for a crowd."

4 to 6 cups chopped chicken (cooked)
2 10½-ounce cans cream of mushroom soup
1 can tomatoes
½ pound sharp New York cheese (grated)
½ cup sliced stuffed olives
2 4-ounce cans of mushrooms (stems and pieces)
1 12-ounce package of spaghetti

Cook spaghetti in chicken broth and drain. Mix all ingredients with spaghetti and put in a casserole dish. Save a little cheese to sprinkle on top. When ready to serve heat at 350 degrees approximately 3 minutes. Serves 14.

Mrs. Henry M. Burt (Lucy)

CHICKEN SPECTACULAR

1 large chicken, cooked, deboned, diced
1 16-ounce can French green beans, seasoned, drained
1 6-ounce box Uncle Ben's curried rice
1 8-ounce can water chestnuts, sliced
1 small onion or 3 tablespoons, chopped
1 10½-ounce can cream of celery soup
1 cup mayonnaise
1 small jar pimiento
Salt to taste

In a covered boiler cook rice in 2½ cups plus 2 tablespoons chicken broth for 20 minutes. Add onions and cook for 5 minutes more. Stir rice occasionally. Add other ingredients to rice and pour into large greased casserole dish. Bake at 350 degrees for 40 minutes to 1 hour until brown. Serves 8-10.

Mrs. R. E. Mullins (Jo Ann)
Mrs. James W. Heacock, Sr. (Becky)
Similar recipes submitted by:
Mrs. Jackie Stephens (Elaine)
Mrs. Carl Reaves (Joyce)

CHICKEN CASSEROLE

"Great for family or guests."

3 large chicken breasts (6 halves)
2 10½-ounce cans cream of chicken soup
1 pint sour cream
1 package Ritz crackers (out of 3 package box)
1½ sticks margarine
2 teaspoons poppy seed

Cook chicken. Cut up into small pieces and arrange in buttered 7½ x 11-inch casserole. Mix soup with sour cream and pour over chicken. Crush crackers and mix with poppy seeds. Sprinkle over chicken. Pour melted butter evenly over other ingredients. Bake at 350 degrees for 25-30 minutes. Serves 6-8.

Mrs. Steve Syer (Marion)
Similar recipe submitted by Mrs. Robert Wikle (Bernice)

CHICKEN LOAF WITH MUSHROOM SAUCE

"Plan an evening with your favorite friends."

1 4-pound chicken
1 cup rice, cooked
4 eggs, well beaten
2 cups bread crumbs
1½ teaspoon salt
3 cups chicken stock

Stew chicken, remove meat from bones and dice. Combine all ingredients and pour into an oiled 10-inch loaf pan. Set in pan of hot water and bake uncovered for 1 hour at 300 degrees. Remove from pan and serve with mushroom sauce. Serves 8-10.

Mushroom Sauce:

¼ cup butter
1 cup mushrooms, sliced
¼ cup flour
2 cups chicken stock
¼ cup rich milk
⅛ teaspoon paprika
½ teaspoon parsley, chopped
½ teaspoon lemon juice
Salt and pepper

Melt butter and add mushrooms. Simmer 5 minutes. Add flour and blend. Gradually add stock and blend. Cook until smooth, stirring constantly. Add milk, paprika, parsley, lemon juice, salt and pepper. Slice loaf and pour sauce over slices when served. The loaf can be frozen, but the sauce should be fresh.

Mrs. George Jones (Alice)

POULÉT ROSE-MARIE

2 whole chicken breasts, split, skinned and lightly salted
¼ cup butter
1 cup mushrooms, sliced
¼ cup flour
1½ cups chicken broth
¼ teaspoon black pepper
Generous dash crushed thyme and rosemary
1 clove garlic, crushed
½ cup light cream
Cooked rice
Toasted almonds

In large skillet, brown chicken in butter; remove. Brown mushrooms; remove. Lower heat. Stir in flour, slowly add broth; stir in garlic and seasonings; add chicken and mushrooms. Cover. Cook over low heat 45 minutes, stirring occasionally. Blend in cream; heat slowly. Serve with rice; garnish with toasted almonds. Preparation time 1½ hours. Serves 4.
Mrs. O. V. Hill, Jr. (Carolyn)

BARBECUED CHICKEN

"Superior oven-barbecued chicken with a nippy sauce."

2 ½ to 3 pound fryers
3 medium onions, peeled and thinly sliced
Salt and pepper

Heat oven to 350 degrees. Clean and dry fryers. Cut in halves lengthwise or quarters. Arrange in single layer, skin side up in a roasting pan. Sprinkle with a little salt and pepper; pour in enough hot water to cover bottom of pan — no more. Arrange onions on fryers, tucking a few under wings and legs. Bake uncovered at 350 degrees for 30 minutes. Turn. Bake 30 minutes more.

Sauce:

2 teaspoons salt
¼ teaspoon pepper
1½ cups tomato juice
¼ teaspoon cayenne pepper
¼ teaspoon dry mustard
4½ teaspoons Worcestershire
1 bay leaf
¾ cup vinegar
1 teaspoon sugar
1 tablespoon brown sugar (optional)
3 cloves garlic, peeled and minced
3 tablespoons butter, margarine or salad oil

Combine all ingredients and simmer 10 minutes. When fryers have baked for one hour, remove from oven; pour off all but ¾ cup of liquid. Turn fryers, skin side up; pour on sauce. Bake 1 hour longer, or until fork can be inserted easily in leg, basting often with sauce in pan. Sauce can be made while chicken is baking or day before. Serves 4-6.
Mrs. George Wooten (Jane)

CREAMED CHICKEN ON CORNMEAL MUFFINS

4 stalks celery, chopped
1 large onion, chopped
¼ cup bell pepper, chopped (optional)
1 small jar pimento, chopped (optional)
4 tablespoons butter
6 tablespoons flour
2 cups chicken broth
Worcestershire sauce to taste
3 to 4 cups chopped chicken or turkey
1 package dry chicken broth
1 can water chestnuts (sliced)
Salt and pepper to taste
Paprika

In skillet sauté celery, onion, bell pepper and pimento until tender in butter. Stir in flour, chicken broth, and Worcestershire to taste. Cook slowly until mixture starts to thicken. Add chicken, packaged broth, water chestnuts, and salt and pepper to taste. Cook until mixture thickens, stirring occasionally. Serve over corn muffins. Sprinkle with paprika, if desired.

Corn Muffins:

Shortening
1 cup corn meal
1 cup sifted all-purpose flour
1 teaspoon salt
2½ teaspoons baking powder
1 cup milk
2 egg yolks
2 egg whites, beaten stiffly

Place ¼ teaspoon shortening in each cup of a 12-cup muffin tin. Heat at 350 degrees until shortening is sizzling. Sift into mixing bowl corn meal, flour, salt and baking powder. Beat together milk and egg yolks and mix into corn meal mixture. Fold in beaten egg whites. Pour hot shortening from tins into mixing bowl and mix. Fill tins no more than two-thirds full and bake at 350 degrees for 20 minutes. This makes 12 large muffins. Mixture may also be baked in an 8 x 10-inch pan to which 2 tablespoons of shortening has been added. Cut into squares and serve.
Mrs. Jim Preuitt (Rona)

POULET MARENGO

"Chalk up points for yourself, when you put this on the table."

4 chicken breasts
½ cup butter
3 tablespoons sherry
½ pound mushrooms
3 tablespoons flour
½ cup chicken stock
2 tablespoons tomato paste
1 bay leaf
2 tablespoons fresh chives, chopped
½ teaspoon salt
2 packages frozen lobster tails
1 pound shrimp
1 onion, sliced
1 teaspoon celery seed
4 medium tomatoes, peeled and sliced

Skin and split chicken breasts. Salt and pepper each piece. Heat butter in large skillet until it begins to foam. Add chicken, brown until golden. Spoon sherry over chicken. Cook three minutes longer on each side. Place chicken in shallow baking dish. Cover with foil and bake in slow oven (approximately 300 degrees) until tender. Sauté mushrooms in butter until tender. Add more butter if necessary. Blend in flour, add chicken stock and simmer. Add tomato paste, bay leaf, chives, salt and pepper. Simmer until tender. Meanwhile, cook frozen lobster tails. Cook shrimp with two quarts of water, containing 1 sliced onion, celery seed and salt. Simmer for 5 minutes. Dash in cold water. Remove meat from lobster shells and cut into bite size pieces. Remove shrimp from shell. Add lobster, shrimp and tomatoes to sauce. Simmer for 5 minutes, just until tomatoes and meat are heated through. Serve chicken breasts on large dish, topped with sauce. Could serve on bed of rice if you like.
Mrs. Hardy Conner (Becky)

CHICKEN CHOW MEIN

"A simple to make people pleaser."

2½ cups cubed cooked chicken
2 tablespoons butter
2 cups thinly sliced celery
1½ cups sliced onions
⅛ teaspoon pepper
1 teaspoon salt
2 cups chicken broth
½ can chestnuts, sliced
1 16-ounce can bean sprouts
1 4-ounce can sliced mushrooms, drained
2 tablespoons cornstarch
3 tablespoons soy sauce

Cook chicken and cube. Add next six ingredients (butter, celery, onions, salt, pepper, and broth). Cook covered about 15 minutes (or until celery and onions are just tender). Add drained chestnuts, bean sprouts, and mushrooms. Heat to boiling. Add cornstarch mixed with soy sauce. Simmer 2 minutes. Serve over rice and top with Chinese noodles and added soy sauce, if desired. Serves 6.
Mrs. Stan Thornton (Cathy)

CURRIED CHICKEN WITH RICE

5 tablespoons butter
½ cup minced onion
1 cup celery, chopped
6 tablespoons flour
2½ tablespoons curry powder
1¼ teaspoon salt
1½ teaspoon sugar
¼ teaspoon ground ginger
1 chicken bouillon cube
1 cup boiling water
2 cups milk
1 teaspoon fresh lemon juice
4 cups chicken, cooked and chopped
Hot cooked rice

Melt butter over low heat. Add onions and celery. Simmer until tender. Stir in flour, curry powder, salt, sugar and ginger. Dissolve bouillon in boiling water, adding this and milk to above mixture. Cook over low heat until mixture thickens, stirring occasionally. Add lemon juice and chopped chicken. Cook mixture until thoroughly heated. Serve hot with cooked rice. Serves 6-8.
Mrs. Charles H. Johnson (Jo Anna)

TEXAS CHICKEN

"You'll use this over and over again."

8 to 10 tortillas
2 cups chicken broth
3 cups cooked chicken, diced
1 can cream of mushroom soup
1 can cream of chicken soup
1 10-ounce can tomatoes with chilies
1 medium onion, chopped and sautéed
3 Jalapeno peppers, cut in thin rings
Garlic powder to taste
Seasoned salt to taste
½ pound sharp cheese, grated

Soak tortillas in chicken broth until broth is absorbed. Spread tortillas over bottom of 9 x 13-inch lightly greased baking dish. Add layers as follow: chicken, mushroom soup, chicken soup, tomatoes with chilies, sautéed onion, jalapeno peppers, garlic powder, seasoned salt. Top with grated cheese. Bake in 350 degree oven 15-20 minutes or until cheese is melted and the mixture is thoroughly heated. Serves 8-10.
Mrs. W. H. Camp, Jr. (Betty Lou)

CURRIED ORANGE CHICKEN

"This is a favorite recipe in London in stately homes."

1 cup English style orange marmalade
1 tablespoon curry powder
1 teaspoon salt
½ cup water
1 broiler-fryer cut into best serving pieces (no back or wings)

Place chicken pieces, cut side down in a buttered 9 x 13-inch baking dish. Combine marmalade, curry powder, salt and water. Spoon this mixture over chicken and bake, uncovered, at 350 degrees for 45 minutes (or longer). Baste several times during cooking. If sauce thickens, add a bit of water. Remove chicken. Pour out sauce and skim off fat. Serve sauce hot with chicken over buttered noodles or rice. Garnish with parsley. This can be prepared ahead and reheated, but not good for freezing.
Mrs. C. P. Eldred (Fess)

game

ONION ROASTED VENISON

4 pound rump or shoulder venison roast
Cooking fat
Salt and pepper
1 package dry onion soup mix
½ cup water

Brown roast in fat on all sides on stove top. Season with salt and pepper. Place in roasting pan and sprinkle onion soup mix on and around roast. Add water. Tightly cover and cook in 300 degree oven until tender, approximately 3½ hours.
Mrs. Larkin Coker (Joan)

DOVE PIE

"This recipe never fails to delight."

12 to 14 doves
Salt water
3 tablespoons Worcestershire sauce
1 stick butter
Salt and pepper to taste
1 pie crust stick or frozen pie crust, slightly thawed
1 4-ounce can of sliced mushrooms (optional)

Soak doves in cold, salt water for an hour to lessen "game taste". Drain. Using a 10 inch skillet, brown doves in butter and Worcestershire sauce. Salt and pepper to taste. Fill with water and simmer on low. Keep refilling as doves cook down. Cook three hours or until doves are almost falling apart. For a thicker gravy, blend 1 tablespoon of flour into juice. Cool and place gravy or juice and doves in a 2-quart casserole. Cover with pie crust made by directions on box. Bake at 400 degrees for 20 minutes until crust is done and doves are hot. Serves 6.
Mrs. W.B. McGehee, III (Evelyn)

KINGDOM-COME DUCK

4 ducks
2 apples, sliced
Celery
2 cans consomme, undiluted
1 can water
Cooked, crumbled bacon

Stuff ducks with apples and celery. Place breast down in baking pan. Add consomme and water. Cover tightly and cook for 3 hours at 350 degrees. Duck should be very tender. Slice breast away. Place duck breast in greased, shallow casserole. Pour sauce over duck; cover and bake at 350 degrees just until hot.

Sauce:

1½ cups butter
⅔ cup sherry
½ cup bourbon
1 5-ounce jar currant jelly
4 tablespoons Worcestershire sauce
Flour (if needed)

In saucepan, melt butter; add sherry, bourbon, Worcestershire sauce and jelly. If too thin, thicken with a little flour. Serves 6-8.
Mrs. Tom B. Bailey Little Rock, Ark.

FRICASSEE OF VENISON

Venison
2 tablespoons butter
Salt and pepper
1 onion, chopped
1 tablespoon parsley, chopped
Beefstock
8-ounces red wine
1 4-ounce can mushrooms, thinly sliced
Flour

Cut venison into cutlets, bite size. Fry gently in butter. Put in baking dish; sprinkle with salt, pepper, onions and parsley. Cover with beef stock and simmer in oven at 325 degrees for 2 hours or until tender. (It can be cooked in crock pot.) 10 minutes before serving add wine and mushrooms. Thicken sauce with flour.
Mrs. Otis R. Burton, Jr. (Louise)

VENISON ROAST

2 bay leaves
6 large onions, quartered
6 large potatoes, quartered
1 venison roast, 8 to 10 pounds
2 packages Lipton Onion Soup mix
Margarine, salt, pepper

Pierce venison with sharp knife in several places. Boil 30 minutes with bay leaves, onions and potatoes. Remove meat; do not wash. Throw away vegetables. Put soup mix in bottom of roasting pan adding enough water to dissolve mix thoroughly. Fill holes in meat with margarine. Salt and pepper generously. Place meat in pan, cover and cook in moderate (325-375 degree) oven 30 minutes per pound.
Mrs. Tom B. Bailey Little Rock, Ark.

DELUXE QUAIL

"What a wonderful flavor."

6 quail
¼ cup butter
¼ cup onion, chopped
¼ cup celery, chopped
1 tablespoon cornstarch
1 cup chicken bouillon
¼ cup cooking sherry
1 tablespoon parsley

Sauté quail in butter for 10 minutes; remove quail. Add onion and celery to butter and cook for 5 minutes over medium heat. Dissolve cornstarch in hot bouillon. Stir into onion-celery mixture and cook until thickened. Stir in sherry and parsley. Arrange quail in shallow pan. Cover with sauce and bake at 350 degrees for 60 minutes.
Mrs. Ronnie Busby (Kay)

meats

CORNED BEEF AND CABBAGE

4 to 5 pounds brisket of beef, mild, cured
3 onions, sliced
3 cloves, whole
6 peppercorns
1 bay leaf
1 clove garlic, peeled and quartered
1 stalk celery
1 carrot, peeled
2 sprigs parsley
6 potatoes, pared and quartered
5 carrots, pared and chunked
1 medium head cabbage, quartered
3 small turnips (optional)

Wipe meat with damp cloth, place in large pan and cover with cold water. Add next 8 ingredients, cover and bring to boil. Reduce heat to low and simmer 3½ to 5 hours or until meat is tender. Remove any scum which appears. About 45 minutes before beef is done, add potatoes, carrots, and turnips if desired. Cover and boil 15 minutes. Add cabbage. Cook until all vegetables are tender. Remove meat and slice. Arrange vegetables on platter around meat and put gravy in gravy boat. Horseradish sauce or mustard is good to serve with meat. Leftover meat makes excellent sandwiches. Preparation time is 6 hours. Serves 6.
Mrs. Larry Barksdale (Fran)

VEAL PARMIGIANA

"Marvelous flavor."

1/3 cup butter, melted
3/4 teaspoon salt
1/8 teaspoon pepper
1 cup cracker crumbs
1/2 cup Parmesan cheese, grated
2 eggs, slightly beaten
6 veal cutlets or steaks
2 8-ounce cans tomato sauce
2 teaspoons oregano
1/4 teaspoon onion salt
1/2 teaspoon sugar
6 slices Mozzarella cheese

Preheat oven to 400 degrees. Put melted butter in 9 x 13 x 2-inch dish or pan. Blend salt, pepper, cracker crumbs, and grated Parmesan in bowl. Beat eggs in separate dish. Dip meat into eggs and coat with crumb mixture. Repeat process. Place meat in buttered baking dish and bake at 400 degrees for 20 minutes. Turn meat and bake 20 minutes longer. Mix tomato sauce, oregano, onion salt, and sugar in sauce pan. Heat. Pour sauce over meat and top with cheese slices. Return to oven for 3 to 5 minutes or until cheese is melted. Preparation time is 1 hour. Excellent served with spaghetti or rice. May be frozen. Serves 6.
Mrs. Larry Barksdale (Fran)

GREEK LEG OF LAMB

"Savor the delightful aroma when you bring this to the table."

1 4 to 5 pound leg of lamb
Salt and pepper to taste
2 garlic cloves, minced
1/4 pound butter
2 pounds pearl onions, peeled and parboiled
2 tablespoons parsley, chopped
2 tablespoons fresh mint, chopped
1 cup white wine
1/2 cup olive oil
Juice of 2 lemons
1 tablespoon oregano

Wash and dry lamb. Rub with salt, pepper, and garlic. Melt 1/4 pound butter in deep skillet and brown gently until crisp on all sides. Remove lamb, strain and reserve butter. Brush large double sheet of foil with butter and place lamb in the center. Meanwhile, sauté parboiled onions until golden brown in 3 tablespoons butter with parsley, mint, salt, and pepper. Surround the lamb with pearl onions and brush pan juices from the onions and the reserved butter from the lamb over the leg. Pour wine, olive oil, and lemon juice over the lamb. Sprinkle with oregano. Fold foil around lamb and seal tightly. Place in greased roasting pan in 375 degree oven for 3 hours. Bring lamb to table in foil on platter.
Mrs. Robert P. Mallis   Atlanta, Georgia

MOUSSAKA

"Greek National Dish"

1 medium eggplant
1 pound chuck, ground
1 cup onion, chopped
¼ cup Burgundy wine
¼ cup water
2 tablespoons parsley, snipped
1 tablespoon tomato paste
1 teaspoon salt
Dash of pepper
1 slice bread, crumbled
2 eggs, beaten
¼ cup sharp cheese, shredded
Dash of cinnamon
¼ cup Parmesan cheese, grated

Pare eggplant and cut into slices ½ inch thick. Sprinkle with salt and dry later with paper towel. In skillet, brown meat with onions. Drain off fat. Add wine, water, parsley, tomato paste, salt, and pepper. Simmer until liquid is nearly absorbed. Cool. Stir in half bread crumbs, eggs, sharp cheese, and cinnamon. Brown eggplant slices on both sides in a little hot oil. Sprinkle bottom of 8 x 11 x 2-inch baking dish with remaining bread crumbs. Cover with a layer of eggplant slices. Spoon on meat mixture. Add remaining eggplant slices. Pour sauce (see below) over all. Top with Parmesan cheese. Bake at 350 degrees for 45 minutes. Serve hot. Serves 6-8.

Sauce:

3 tablespoons butter
3 tablespoons flour
1½ cups milk
½ teaspoon salt
Dash pepper and nutmeg
1 egg, beaten

In saucepan, melt butter; stir in flour. Add milk; cook and stir until thick and bubbly. Add salt, pepper, and nutmeg. Add a small amount of this sauce to egg; mix; then add to hot mixture. Cook low for two minutes, stirring constantly.

Mrs. Alton James Mobile, Alabama

BO'S BEEF

"Do this today and serve tomorrow."

3 pounds sirloin, cubed bite-size
3 medium onions, chopped
¾ pound mushrooms
3 cups beef bouillon
1 teaspoon Accent
3 tablespoons Worcestershire sauce
5 tablespoons soy sauce
3 dashes Tabasco
1 teaspoon salt
2 dashes pepper
1½ cups red wine
6 tablespoons cornstarch, dissolved in water

Sauté onions in 2 tablespoons of butter. Remove from pan. Brown beef cubes (add more butter if necessary) and add mushrooms that have been sauteed. Add onions, beef stock, and seasonings. Cook slowly for 15 minutes. Add wine and cornstarch. Cook until thickened. Omit the wine when freezing. Add when reheating. Serve over rice. Serves 8-10.
Mrs. Kenneth Power (Dot)
Similar recipe submitted by Mrs. Bill Perry (Linda)

BEEF KABOB

3 medium green peppers
3 medium tomatoes
1 large jar whole mushrooms
2 large onions
3½ pounds sirloin roast or sirloin steak, cubed

Cut all vegetables except mushrooms into chunk size. Place together in large bowl.

Marinade:

2 cups vegetable oil
4 tablespoons garlic juice
1⅔ cups lemon juice
½ cup onion, grated finely
1½ teaspoons thyme
1 tablespoon oregano

Combine all marinade ingredients in large jar and shake well. Pour ⅓ to ½ marinade over meat and marinate for 5 hours in refrigerator. Pour remaining marinade over vegetables and marinate for 2 hours. Alternate meat and vegetables on skewers up to 1 hour before cooking. Cook on grill until kabobs reach desired doneness. Amount and types of vegetables may be varied to suit taste. Serves 8.
Mrs. Stan Thornton (Cathy)

MARINATED STEAK

3 pounds round steak, 1½ inches thick
1 teaspoon ginger
1 teaspoon dry mustard
1 teaspoon Accent
1 teaspoon garlic powder
1 tablespoon sugar
½ cup soy sauce
½ cup salad oil

Place steak in large plastic bag. Mix other ingredients together and pour into bag. Close end of bag tightly. Place in refrigerator for 24 hours. Turn bag over 3 or 4 times during marinating period. Pour off marinade and save. Cook meat over charcoal fire for 20 minutes on each side for rare meat. Serve with rice. Spoon marinade over meat and rice.
Mrs. Merrill Sweat (Barbara)

RARE RIB ROAST IN ROCK SALT

"Great with a sour cream-horseradish sauce."

4-6 pound rib roast
4-6 boxes rock salt
Foil to line roaster
Worcestershire sauce
Ground pepper

Preheat oven to 500 degrees. Wipe roast with damp cloth. Season with salt, pepper, and Worcestershire sauce. Line roaster with foil. Cover bottom of pan with rock salt. Put in meat and completely cover with rock salt. Sprinkle with water to seal. Cook 15 minutes per pound at 500 degrees. To remove meat, break salt crust and allow meat to sit for 10 minutes. Slice and serve.
Mrs. Tommy Robbs (Boo)

BEEF BURGUNDY

"A tasty and elegant dish for special occasions."

4½ to 5 pounds top round of beef
3 tablespoons Crisco
1½ cups Burgundy
½ cup green olives, pitted
1 or 2 carrots, cut up
1 small can mushrooms
1 Reynolds brown in bag

Brown meat. Sear in pan on top of stove in Crisco. Place meat in bag according to directions on bag. Add drippings, burgundy, olives, carrots, and mushrooms. Cook at 250 degrees from 4-6 hours according to how well done you desire. Serves 8-10.
Mrs. John Coleman (Mary Dowdell)

BEEF ORIENTAL

1 pound top round steak, cut in strips
2 tablespoons salad oil
2 tablespoons soy sauce
2 tablespoons dry sherry
3 tablespoons cornstarch
½ tablespoon sugar
3 cups onion rings, thinly sliced
1 small can mushrooms
1 16-ounce can bean sprouts
1 box Uncle Ben's rice
3 tablespoons soy sauce

Heat 2 tablespoons salad oil, 2 tablespoons soy sauce, sherry, cornstarch and sugar in small saucepan. Cook onion for a few minutes until clear but not brown. Dip steak strips in this mixture and drop in a skillet of hot oil until brown. Add mushrooms and beef to sauce and onions. Serve over rice. Top with bean sprouts and 3 tablespoons of soy sauce.
over rice.
Mrs. Paul Quenelle (Peggy)

NEW ORLEANS HAMBURGER

1 pound ground beef
1 cup onion, chopped
4 tablespoons mustard
4 tablespoons catsup
1 can chicken gumbo soup
Salt and pepper to taste

Brown meat in skillet and drain. Add all other ingredients, mix well and simmer for 15 to 20 minutes. Serve on toasted hamburger buns. May be served open face. Serves 6-8.
Mrs. Mary Corlew

BEEF AND POTATO CASSEROLE

2 strips bacon
4 medium potatoes, thinly sliced
1 teaspoon salt
¼ teaspoon pepper
2 tablespoons butter
1 medium onion, chopped
1 pound ground beef
1 16-ounce can spaghetti sauce

Cook bacon. Add potatoes thinly sliced. Cover and cook slowly for 10 minutes. Sprinkle with ½ of salt and pepper. Place in casserole dish. Melt butter. Add chopped onion and meat. Cook until meat loses redness. Add remaining salt and pepper. Pour over mixture in casserole dish. Cover with spaghetti sauce and cook 45 minutes in 350 degree oven. Serves 4-6.
Mrs. George Hartsfield (Linda)

STIFATHO

"Greek Stew"

- **3 pounds finest cut beef stew meat cut into 1½ inch pieces**
- **1 tablespoon cooking oil**
- **2 teaspoons salt**
- **¼ teaspoon pepper**
- **18 small onions, peeled**
- **1 6-ounce can tomato paste**
- **¼ cup vinegar**
- **2 tablespoons raisins (optional)**
- **1 tablespoon brown sugar, packed**
- **¼ teaspoon ground cumin**
- **1 clove garlic, minced**
- **1 bay leaf**
- **1 1-inch stick cinnamon**

In 4-quart kettle, combine meat, oil, salt, and pepper. Toss well but do not brown. Top with onions. In bowl combine tomato paste, vinegar raisins, sugar, cumin, and garlic. Add to stew along with bay leaf and cinnamon. (Do not stir.) Cover and bake in 250 degree oven 4 to 5 hours or until meat is tender. You may use slow cooker set at low for 8 to 10 hours or on high for 5 to 6 hours until meat is fork tender. Skim off fat and discard bay leaf and cinnamon stick. Delicious over rice or spaghetti. Serves 6.

Mrs. C. P. Eldred (Fess)

TENNESSEE HOT POT

- **2 tablespoons oil**
- **2 tablespoons butter**
- **2 cloves garlic, crushed**
- **3 medium onions, chopped**
- **1 pound beef, cubed small**
- **1 pound pork, cubed small**
- **2 teaspoons salt**
- **Black pepper**
- **½ teaspoon dry mustard**
- **½ teaspoon cayenne pepper**
- **1 10½-ounce can bouillon**
- **2 10-ounce cans tomato purée**
- **2 tablespoons vinegar**
- **1 teaspoon chili powder**
- **⅛ teaspoon ginger**
- **1 tablespoon Worcestershire sauce**
- **1 tablespoon lemon juice**
- **2 tablespoons soy sauce**
- **1 bay leaf**
- **⅛ teaspoon cloves, ground**
- **⅛ teaspoon oregano, dried**
- **⅛ teaspoon thyme, dried**
- **1½ tablespoons parsley**
- **1 teaspoon liquid smoke**

Heat oil and butter in heavy Dutch oven. Add garlic and onions and saute until yellow. Remove to paper towels and drain. Place meat in pot and sear quickly, adding salt and pepper while browning. Return onions and garlic to pot. Add all other ingredients. Stir well, cover, and simmer 3 hours. If mixture cooks down, add small amount of water. This dish should be made a day ahead so flavors will mellow and fat can be skimmed from the surface. Serves 8-10.

Mrs. Lewis Anderson   Mobile, Alabama

BEEF BEER-B-CUE

2 pounds top round steak, 1 $1/2$ inch thick
2 tablespoons Accent
1 12-ounce can beer
2 beef bouillon cubes
1 cup hot water
3 cloves garlic, minced
2 tablespoons molasses
1 $1/2$ teaspoons salt
8 peppercorns
1 teaspoon oregano
1 large onion, sliced

Score steak on both sides. Sprinkle Accent on both sides. Prepare charcoal on grill allowing time for coals to get gray. Allow enough charcoal for a cooking time of 2 $1/2$ hours. Using 25 inch wide heavy duty quilted foil, tear off 50 inches. Fold in half. Place steak in center. Fold foil sharply to make a pan an inch larger than steak. Be careful to make corners leak proof. Dissolve bouillon cube in hot water. In a pitcher mix beer, bouillon, garlic, molasses, salt, peppercorns, and oregano. Pour liquid over steak. Put onion slices on steak. Close foil over top and sides. Place on grill 2 or 3 inches above coals. Cook 2 hours. Remove to a pan in order to save sauce. Remove foil. Place steak on grill over coals allowing 8-10 minutes on each side to get charcoal flavor. Baste with sauce while on the grill. Place on warm platter with onions on top of steak. Pour remaining sauce over it.
Steve Syer

CAN'T MISS CASSEROLE

1 cup rice, uncooked
Salt and pepper to taste
1 cup canned whole kernel corn
2 8-ounce cans tomato sauce
$1/2$ can water
1 cup onion, chopped
1 cup green pepper, chopped
1 pound ground beef, uncooked
3 strips bacon, uncooked
$1/4$ can water

In a greased 2-quart baking dish combine rice, salt, pepper, corn, 1 can tomato sauce, water, onion, and green pepper. Add ground beef and second can of tomato sauce. Add $1/4$ can of water and cover with bacon strips. Cover and bake at 350 degrees for 1 hour. Uncover and bake for 30 minutes or until bacon is crisp. Serves 4-6.
Mrs. Buddy Wesley (Ann)

DAUBE CREOLE

1½ cups onions, finely chopped
2 tablespoons parsley
1½ bay leaves, crushed
2 teaspoons salt
1½ teaspoons pepper
¼ teaspoon dried thyme leaves
¼ teaspoon cloves
¼ pound salt pork or bacon
6½ pounds boneless beef round roast
2 tablespoons salad oil
2 10½-ounce cans beef broth
1 cup sherry

In small bowl combine ½ cup onion, parsley, bay leaves, salt, pepper, thyme, and cloves. Mix well. Cut salt pork into strips 3 inches long and ¼ inch thick. Roll in onion mixture. Wipe roast with damp cloth. Make cuts 3-4 inches deep and 1½ inches apart. Push salt pork into cuts. Preheat oven to 325 degrees. In hot oil using Dutch oven, brown roast on all sides. Add remaining onion mixture, beef broth, and sherry. Cook with a cover for 1 hour. Uncover and roast, basting occasionally for 2-2½ hours or until tender. Remove roast to platter. Skim excess fat from pan juices. Serve juice as gravy. As you serve, remove the seasonings from slits in meat. Serves 8-10.
Mrs. Richard Bliss (Billie)

AZTEC SILVERPLATED POT ROAST

"This recipe should be called Aztec STERLING Pot Roast. It's great."

4 pound eye round roast
Salt and pepper to taste
Tenderizer
1 medium onion, chopped
1 medium green pepper, chopped
2 cloves garlic, minced
2 tablespoons butter
2 tablespoons flour
1 8-ounce can tomato sauce
⅔ cup beef bouillon
¼ teaspoon basil
1 4-ounce can sliced ripe olives
2 tablespoons parsley, minced
2 tablespoons onion tops, chopped

Slice roast diagonally in ¾ inch slices. Sprinkle each slice with salt, pepper, and tenderizer. Let stand for 30 minutes. Sauté onion, green pepper, and garlic in butter until soft but not brown. Blend in the flour. Add tomato sauce, bouillon, olives, and basil. Heat until almost boiling. Place meat on a four foot length of foil. Pour the sauce over and between the slices and seal securely. Cook at 350 degrees for about 3½ hours. Sprinkle with parsley and onion tops.
Mrs. Hardy Conner (Becky)

STUFFED CABBAGE ROLLS

"A little time consuming – but well worth the effort!"

1 pound ground beef
¼ pound ground pork
2 teaspoons salt
½ teaspoon pepper
¾ cup cooked rice
1 small onion, grated
2 8-ounce cans tomato sauce with mushrooms
12 large cabbage leaves
¼ cup brown sugar
¼ cup freshly squeezed lemon juice or vinegar

Combine meats, salt, pepper, rice, onion, and 1 can tomato sauce. Blanche cabbage leaves by covering them with boiling water for 3-4 minutes. Drain. Place equal portions of meat mixture in center of each cabbage leaf, fold ends over, roll up, and fasten with toothpick. Mix remaining can of tomato sauce with brown sugar and lemon juice and pour over cabbage rolls. Simmer covered for 30 minutes, basting occasionally. Uncover and continue cooking for 30 minutes. Serves 6.
Mrs. Eugene Caldwell (Nell)

FRANKFURTER CASSEROLE

1 pound frankfurters
2 tablespoons butter
½ to 1 cup onions, sliced
1 9-ounce package frozen French cut green beans
1 10¾-ounce can cream of mushroom soup
1 cup milk
½ teaspoon salt
¼ teaspoon marjoram
1 9-ounce can biscuits
½ cup Cheddar cheese, shredded
½ cup Kraft sharp cheese, grated

Cut frankfurters in halves lengthwise, then crosswise and set aside. Melt butter in heavy skillet. Add onions and cook slowly until soft. Separate green beans but do not defrost. Add to onions. Stir in soup, milk, salt, and marjoram. Mix well. Set over low heat until mixture begins to simmer. Fold in frankfurters and simmer for 20 minutes. Remove biscuits from can and separate. Cut each in half and arrange in a border around skillet. Bake at 375 degrees until biscuits are brown. Remove from oven and sprinkle cheese over biscuits. Serve as soon as cheese is melted.
Mrs. Buddy Holcomb (Peggy)

COUNTRY PIE

"Great for a quick family meal."

The Crust:

½ cup Hunt's tomato sauce
½ cup bread crumbs
¼ cup onions, chopped
⅛ teaspoon pepper
¼ cup green pepper, chopped
1 pound lean ground beef
1½ teaspoons salt
⅛ teaspoon oregano

Combine all crust ingredients in a bowl and mix well with a fork. Then pat the meat mixture gently into bottom and sides of a greased 9 inch pie plate.

Filling:

1⅓ cups Minute Rice
1½ 8-ounce cans Hunt's tomato sauce
1 cup water
1 cup Cheddar cheese, grated
½ teaspoon salt

Combine all filling ingredients. Spoon mixture into meat shell. Cover with aluminum foil and bake in moderate oven at 350 degrees for 25 minutes. Uncover and top with remaining cheese. Bake uncovered 10-15 minutes. Serves 5-6.

Mrs. George Wooten (Jane)

GROUND BEEF STROGANOFF

1 8-ounce package small noodles
1½ pounds ground beef
Salt and pepper to taste
2 8-ounce cans tomato sauce
1 4-ounce can sliced mushrooms, drained
1 8-ounce package cream cheese
1 cup cottage cheese
½ cup sour cream
½ cup green onions, chopped
1 tablespoon green pepper, chopped

Cook noodles as directed. Drain. Brown beef keeping it well broken up. Salt and pepper lightly. Stir in mushrooms and tomato sauce and remove from heat. Combine cream cheese, cottage cheese, sour cream, onion, and green pepper. Mix well. Grease 2-quart casserole. Place noodles in bottom of dish. Combine meat and sour cream mixture. Pour over noodles. If desired, sharp cheese may be sprinkled over top. Place in 350 degree oven for 30 minutes. Serves 6-8.

Mrs. Erskine Murray (Betty)

ARTICHOKE AND CHIPPED BEEF

"A wonderful idea for a bridge luncheon."

1 8-ounce jar chipped beef
3 tablespoons butter
1 tablespoon all-purpose flour
1 10¾-ounce can cream of mushroom soup
1 8-ounce carton sour cream
½ cup dry white wine
2 tablespoons Parmesan cheese, grated
Dash of Tabasco
1 14-ounce can artichokes, drained and sliced
4 frozen patty shells

Separate beef and sauté in butter. Stir in flour, mushroom soup, sour cream, wine, cheese and Tabasco. Stir and simmer until bubbly. Add artichokes and simmer again. Serve in patty shells. Serves 4.
Mrs. A. B. Brown (Mary)

LASAGNE

"A great stand-by recipe."

1½ pounds ground beef
1 clove garlic
3 tablespoons parsley
½ teaspoon salt
2 16-ounce cans tomatoes
2 6-ounce cans tomato paste
1 6-ounce jar sliced mushrooms
1 10-ounce package noodles
2 12-ounce cartons cottage cheese
2 eggs, beaten
2 teaspoons salt
½ teaspoon pepper
½ cup Parmesan cheese
1 pound Mozzarella cheese, grated

Brown ground beef with garlic. Add 1 tablespoon of parsley, salt, tomatoes, tomato paste, and mushrooms. Simmer 45 minutes. Cook noodles and drain. Mix cottage cheese, eggs, salt, pepper, 2 tablespoons parsley, and Parmesan cheese. In 13 x 9 x 2-inch baking dish, alternate layers beginning with noodles, then cottage cheese, then Mozzarella and finally meat mixture. Repeat. Bake at 375 degrees for 30 minutes. Lasagne may be refrigerated 1 day or may be frozen. Takes 1½ hours from start to finish. Serves 8.
Mrs. Steve Syer (Marion)
Similar recipe submitted by Mrs. Buddy Wesley (Ann)

TERIYAKI POT ROAST

"This roast is delicious served with Japanese vegetables."

2 tablespoons flour
1½ teaspoons salt
⅓ teaspoon pepper
½ teaspoon curry powder
3-4 pound beef arm or blade cut roast
3 tablespoons lard or drippings
¼ cup water
¼ cup honey
¼ cup soy sauce
¼ teaspoon ground ginger
¼ cup flour

Combine 2 tablespoons flour, salt, pepper, and curry powder. Dredge meat in seasoned flour. Brown in lard or drippings. Add water, honey, soy sauce, and ground ginger. Cover tightly and cook slowly for 2½ hours or until meat is tender. Add water to cooking liquid to make 2 cups. Thicken with ¼ cup flour for gravy.
Mrs. Guy Kaylor (Florence)

HAMBURGER DISH

"A delicious last minute dish."

1 pound ground chuck
⅔ cup tomato juice
1 cup oatmeal
½ teaspoon garlic salt
2 cups onions, sliced
¼ cup flour
1 beef bouillon cube
2 cups water

Mix first 4 ingredients and make into thick patties (about 6). Brown in small amount of oil and remove. Put in baking dish or electric fry pan. Brown 2 cups sliced onions in same pan meat was cooked in. Add ¼ cup flour and brown. Melt beef bouillon cube in ½ cup hot water. Add 1½ cups water to make 2 cups. Add this to flour mixture and thicken. Pour mixture over patties and cook 20 minutes at 400 degrees. A tossed salad and green peas complete your dinner.
Mrs. Curtis Lackey (Barbara)

OLD FASHIONED GERMAN CHILI

1 block frozen chili
1 pound ground beef
1 small onion, chopped
1 16-ounce can tomatoes
1 8-ounce can tomato purée
1 21-ounce can kidney beans
2 tablespoons chili powder
Dash of salt
1 1-pound box thin spaghetti

Put frozen chili in pan filled with a little water and melt. Brown meat and add onion. Add tomatoes, puree, beans and meat mixture to chili. Add chili powder and salt. Cook for 1 hour. Cook spaghetti until tender and drain. Add to chili mixture and cook until ready to serve.
Mrs. Walter Burt (Brenda)

CHILI

2 cups dried red beans or kidney beans
2 tablespoons salt
1 large onion, whole
1 large bay leaf
1 large clove garlic
2 tablespoons butter
6 cups water
1½ pounds lean ground beef
1 46-ounce can tomato juice
4 tablespoons chili powder
1½ teaspoons ground cumin

Combine in large pot the washed beans and water. Bring to boil for 2 minutes. Cover tightly and let stand overnight. Add salt, onion, bay leaf, garlic, and butter. Bring to boil, reduce heat and simmer for 2 hours or until beans are tender. Lift out onion and bay leaf. Brown meat quickly in another skillet breaking into small pieces. Add to beans. Add about ¾ can of tomato juice to the pan meat was fried in. This will bring up drippings. Add to beans. Measure chili powder and cumin in small bowl and mix into smooth paste using liquid from pan. Add to bean mixture. Bring to boil, reduce heat and simmer for 1-1½ hours. Freezes well. When reheating add more tomato juice.
Mrs. Dennis Ronning Savannah, Georgia

BEEF STROGANOFF

"Splendid for a buffet."

2 pounds boneless beef, tenderloin or sirloin
½ cup flour
1 teaspoon salt
½ teaspoon monosodium glutamate
⅛ teaspoon pepper
⅓ cup butter or margarine
½ cup onion, chopped
2 cups beef broth
1⅓ cups pre-cooked rice
½ pound mushrooms
3 tablespoons butter or margarine
1 cup sour cream
3 tablespoons tomato paste
1 teaspoon Worcestershire sauce

Cut beef into strips. Mix flour, salt, monosodium glutamate, and pepper. Coat meat evenly with flour mixture. Heat butter in heavy skillet. Add meat and onions. Slowly brown meat on all sides. Add meat broth and simmer covered 25 minutes. Cook rice according to directions on package. Clean and slice mushrooms. Heat 3 tablespoons butter in skillet. Add mushrooms and cook until brown and tender. Blend together sour cream, tomato paste, and Worcestershire sauce. Add the sour cream mixture in small amounts to meat, stirring vigorously. Add mushrooms. Return and cook over low heat slowly stirring with spoon until thoroughly heated. Do not boil. Serve over rice. Serves 6.
Mrs. Guy Kaylor (Florence)

PICADILLO

"Something pleasingly different with ground beef."

½ pound ground pork (all beef may be used)
½ pound ground beef
3 tomatoes, diced
3 green onions, chopped
1 medium potato, diced
¾ cup seedless raisins (optional)
1 tablespoon chili powder
¾ cup slivered almonds
1 teaspoon salt
½ teaspoon black pepper
2 cloves garlic, minced
2 Jalapeno peppers, chopped
1 teaspoon oregano

Brown meat. Cover with water and simmer 30 minutes. Add remaining ingredients and cook down. Serve with Fritos as a dip or roll in warm tortillos as an entree. This may be made a few days ahead. Reheat and serve in chafing dish.

Mrs. Dell Hill (Carolyn)
Similar recipe submitted by Mr. George R. Burton

FOOTBALL CASSEROLE

"Keep one of these in the freezer for after the game."

1 pound ground beef
2 tablespoons shortening
1 medium onion, chopped
2 cups canned tomatoes
1 tablespoon catsup
1 tablespoon steak sauce
½ cup green pepper, chopped
2 tablespoons parsley, chopped
1 5-ounce package elbow macaroni
Salt and pepper to taste
1 can cream of mushroom soup
1 cup grated cheese

Brown beef in shortening. Add onions, tomatoes, catsup, steak sauce, green pepper, and parsley. Simmer 30 minutes. Cook macaroni according to directions on package. Drain. Combine macaroni and ground beef mixture in casserole. Season to taste. Gently spoon mushroom soup into mixture. Mix lightly. Sprinkle with grated cheese. Bake at 350 degrees for 30 minutes or until top is bubbling and brown.

Mrs. Alvin Bresler *Birmingham, Alabama*

SWEDISH MEAT BALLS

"What a wonderful flavor."

2 cups soft bread crumbs
1/3 cup milk
1/2 cup onion, chopped
2 pounds ground beef
1 egg, slightly beaten
1/4 teaspoon pepper
2 teaspoons salt
1/2 teaspoon nutmeg
2 tablespoons butter
2 tablespoons flour
1 cup hot water
1 beef bouillon cube
1 8-ounce carton sour cream

Soak bread crumbs in milk. Add onion, ground beef, egg, salt, pepper, and nutmeg. Mix thoroughly and shape into balls about 1 inch in diameter. Brown in butter and remove from heat. Blend flour, water, and bouillon cube in with grease in skillet and add sour cream to mixture. Serve hot over meat balls as gravy.
Mrs. Barry McCrary (Marilyn)

INSTANT PIZZA SPREAD FOR HUNGRY KIDS

2 cups ham or 1 can Spam
1 pound Velveeta cheese
1 large onion
1 6-ounce can tomato paste
4 tablespoons Mazola oil
2 tablespoons oregano
Dash of salt

Grind through meat grinder meat, cheese, and onion. Add remaining ingredients and mix well. Store in refrigerator several hours before serving. Spread on bread, buns, crackers, or leftover biscuits. Place in 250 degree oven for about 15 minutes or until cheese melts and bubbles. This mixture will keep for weeks in refrigerator or may be frozen.
Mrs. William Parker (Dorothy)

GRAPEFRUIT AND BAKED HAM

2 pink grapefruits
3 tablespoons brown sugar
1 tablespoon catsup
1/2 teaspoon Tabasco
1 slice of ham, 1-inch thick

Halve grapefruit and cut sections, removing core if desired. Combine brown sugar, catsup and Tabasco; mix well to make a smooth paste. Spread paste over cut side of the grapefruit halves and on top of the ham slice. Place grapefruit halves and ham in large shallow pan. Bake at 350 degrees for 45 minutes. Serves 4.
Mrs. Ken H. Wallis (Kathy)

GOUGERE WITH MUSHROOMS AND HAM

Paté a Choux:

1 cup sifted all-purpose flour
Pinch each, salt and pepper
1 cup water
½ cup butter, cut up
4 eggs
⅛ pound (½ cup) Cheddar cheese, diced

Sift flour, salt, and pepper on to sheet of waxed paper. Heat water and butter in a large saucepan until butter melts. Turn up heat and bring water to boiling. Add flour mixture all at once and stir vigorously until mixture forms a ball in the center of the pan — about 1 minute. Allow mixture to cool for 5 minutes. Add eggs one at a time, beating well with a wooden spoon after each addition. (This is important as the gougere will not puff otherwise.) Stir in diced cheese.

Filling:

4 tablespoons butter
2 medium onions (1 cup), chopped
½ pound mushrooms, sliced
1½ tablespoons flour
1 teaspoon salt
¼ teaspoon pepper
1 teaspoon instant chicken broth
1 cup hot water
2 large tomatoes, peeled, quartered, and seeded or 2 cups canned tomatoes
6 ounces cooked ham (1½ cups), in strips
2 tablespoons Cheddar cheese, shredded
2 tablespoons of parsley, chopped

Melt butter in a large skillet; sauté onion until soft, but not burned. Add mushrooms and continue cooking for 2 minutes. Sprinkle with flour, salt, and pepper; mix and cook an additional 2 minutes. Add instant chicken broth and water; mix well. Bring to a boil, stirring constantly. Simmer for 4 minutes. Remove sauce from heat. Cut each tomato quarter into 4 strips and add to sauce with ham strips. Taste; add additional seasoning if needed. Butter a 12 x 7 x 2-inch baking dish. Spoon the paté a choux in a ring around the edge leaving the center open. Pour filling into center; sprinkle with cheese. Bake in a 400 degree oven 40 minutes or until puffed and brown and filling is bubbly. Sprinkle with parsley and serve at once. Serves 4-6.
Mrs. Ralph Wallis (Meg)

CHEROKEE CASSEROLE

1 pound ground beef
1 tablespoon olive oil
¾ cup onion, finely chopped
1½ teaspoons salt
Dash of pepper
⅛ teaspoon garlic powder
⅛ teaspoon thyme
⅛ teaspoon oregano
½ bay leaf
1 16-ounce can tomatoes
1 10½-ounce can cream of mushroom soup
1 cup minute rice
6 stuffed olives, sliced
3 slices cheese, cut in ½ inch slices

Brown meat in olive oil. Add onions and cook until tender. Stir in the next ingredients in order given except 3 olives and the cheese. Bring to a boil, reduce heat, and simmer for 5 minutes. Stir occasionally. Spoon into baking dish and top with cheese strips. Broil until cheese is melted. Garnish with sliced olives. Serves 4-6.
Mrs. Joe Upchurch (Frances)

CHEESEBURGER PIE

1 pound ground beef
½ cup catsup
¼ cup onion, chopped
⅛ teaspoon pepper
¾ teaspoon salt
½ teaspoon oregano
½ cup evaporated milk
⅓ cup fine bread crumbs
1 uncooked 9-inch pie shell

Combine all ingredients with hands and place in unbaked pie shell. Bake at 350 degrees for 30 to 45 minutes.

Topping:

4 ounces cheese, grated
1 tablespoon Worcestershire sauce

Combine cheese and Worcestershire sauce and sprinkle on pie. Bake 10 minutes longer. Cool 10 minutes and cut into wedges to serve. Serves 6.
Mrs. Marion Sims (Ginny)

SWISS-TURKEY-HAM BAKE

"Superb – perfect for a ladies lunch."

¾ cup onion, chopped
4½ tablespoons flour
½ teaspoon pepper
3 tablespoons butter
¾ teaspoon salt
1½ cups light cream
1 4-ounce can mushrooms
3 tablespoons dry sherry
2 cups turkey, cooked and cubed
2 cups ham, cooked and cubed
1 4-ounce can water chestnuts, drained and sliced
½ cup Swiss cheese, shredded
1½ cups soft bread crumbs
3 tablespoons butter, melted

Cook onion in 3 tablespoons butter until tender. Blend in flour, salt and pepper. Add undrained mushrooms, cream and sherry. Cook and stir until thickened. Add turkey, ham and water chestnuts. Pour into a 1½-quart casserole. Top with Swiss cheese. Mix crumbs with butter and sprinkle around edges of casserole. Bake at 400 degrees for 25 minutes. Serves 6.

Mrs. Harry G. Moore, Jr. *Signal Mountain, Tennessee*

TIMBALES (HAM OR CHICKEN)

"Ideal for bridal brunch with curried fruit and baked grits."

¼ cup bread crumbs
⅔ cup milk or chicken broth
2 tablespoons butter or oleo
2 teaspoons parsley flakes
2 eggs, well beaten with salt
1 cup ham or chicken, diced or ground

Cook milk (or broth) and bread crumbs to soften. Add butter and cook until melted. Remove from heat and add other ingredients. Pour into buttered custard cups (4 full cups or 8 half-full cups). Cook in "water bath" at 350 degrees for 40 minutes. Unmold and serve with a sauce ladled over timbales.

Sauce for ham timbales:

Undiluted cheese soup with pimentoes added, heated

Sauce for chicken timbales:

Undiluted mushroom soup with mushrooms added, heated

Mrs. Tom Richardson (Elaine)

CANADIAN BACON UPSIDE DOWN CAKE

"A real pleaser for overnight guests' breakfast."

2 6-ounce packages Canadian bacon, sliced
3 tablespoons butter or margarine
1 8¼-ounce can pineapple rings
1 10-ounce package cornbread or corn muffin mix
Maple blended syrup

In large fish skillet melt butter. Remove from heat. Drain pineapple rings well. Place 1 pineapple ring in center of skillet. Arrange bacon slices and remaining pineapple rings, overlapping, around edge of skillet. Prepare corn bread mix as package directs. Spoon batter evenly over bacon and pineapple and bake according to package directions. Immediately invert cake on to heated platter. Cut in wedges and serve with maple syrup. Serves 8.
Mrs. Myron Waits (Miller)

PRESSED HAM ASPIC

1 tablespoon gelatin
¼ cup cold water
½ cup celery, chopped
½ small onion
1 small green pepper
1 pimiento
2 hard cooked eggs
½ cup mayonnaise
1 teaspoon lemon juice
1 teaspoon Worcestershire sauce
¼ cup crackers, crushed
2 cups ground cooked ham

Soak gelatin in cold water. Heat the mixture over hot water. Chop all vegetables very fine. Chop eggs and add all the ingredients to ground ham. Pour in mold and chill. Slice to serve. This may be prepared in advance. Serves 6-8.
Mrs. C. L. Kelley (Hattie)

PORK CHOP DINNER FOR SIX

6 pork chops
Cracker meal
1 egg, beaten
Salt and pepper to taste
4 tablespoons cooking oil
6 tablespoons uncooked rice
1 1-pound can tomatoes, whole
6 onion rings
6 bell pepper rings
1 can chicken broth

Batter pork chops in cracker meal, egg, and again in cracker meal. Brown in hot cooking oil. Salt and pepper to taste. Place chops on paper towel and wipe skillet clean of grease. Place pork chops back in skillet. Top each with tablespoon uncooked rice, 1 tablespoon tomatoes, 1 onion ring, and 1 bell pepper ring. Salt again and pour chicken broth over chops. Cook slowly for 1 hour, covered. Baste during cooking time with juice.
Mrs. Joe Wallis (Dorothy)

SWEET AND SOUR PORK RIBS

"Very good, with a different taste."

8 country style ribs
1 tablespoon soy sauce

Parboil ribs then brush with soy sauce. Bake in 400 degree oven for 1 hour or until done.

Sauce:

½ cup sugar
½ cup vinegar
1 teaspoon ginger
¼ cup red wine
1 tablespoon cornstarch

Mix all ingredients for sauce except cornstarch. Heat over low heat until it boils. Slowly add cornstarch mixed with water, so as not to lump, and continue cooking for 1 minute. Pour over cooked ribs. Serve with rice.
Mr. Bob Cunningham

CREOLE PORK CHOPS

4 pork chops, ¾ inch thick
1 tablespoon shortening
1 1-pound can tomatoes, chopped with juice
1 medium green pepper, seeded and cut in strips
1 cup celery, sliced
1 teaspoon salt
½ teaspoon poultry seasoning
4 tablespoons uncooked rice

Remove fat from chops. Brown in shortening. Add tomatoes, green pepper, celery, salt and poultry seasoning. Cover and cook 10 minutes. Top each pork chop with 1 tablespoon rice and spoon tomato juice on top. Cover and cook slowly for 1 hour. Baste rice occasionally with juice. This makes a complete meal served with corn muffins and salad.
Mrs. Ed Christenberry (Frances)
Similar recipe submitted by Misses Toni and Nora Hardiman
Birmingham, Alabama

HAM LOAF

"Try this on company."

1½ pounds ham
¾ pound pork
2 cups fine bread crumbs
2 eggs, beaten

Grind ham and pork together. Mix in other ingredients and shape into small loaves. Bake in greased pan at 350 degrees for 1 hour. Turn loaves occasionally and baste with sauce.

Sauce:

1 cup brown sugar
1 teaspoon dry mustard
¼ cup vinegar
6 to 8 cloves
1 cinnamon stick

Mix together and boil 1 minute.
Miss Elizabeth Barnes

SWEET AND SOUR PORK

1½ pounds lean pork, ½ by 2 inch strips
2 tablespoons fat
¼ cup water
2 green peppers, cut in strips
1 large onion, thinly sliced
1 20-ounce can pineapple chunks
¼ cup vinegar
2 tablespoons soy sauce
1 teaspoon salt
¼ cup brown sugar
2 tablespoons cornstarch

Brown pork in melted fat in skillet over medium heat. Add water, peppers, and onion. Simmer 1 hour or until tender. Water may need to be added. Add pineapple, vinegar, soy sauce, salt and brown sugar mixed with cornstarch. Cook until thickened.
Mrs. Henry Rush (Selena)
Similar recipe submitted by Mrs. Jim Davis (Becky)

sauces

JEZEBEL SAUCE

1 12-ounce jar pineapple preserves
1 5-ounce jar Coleman's mustard
1 12-ounce jar apple jelly
1 5-ounce jar horseradish
Salt to taste
Freshly ground black pepper to taste

Combine all ingredients with an electric mixer. Keeps indefinitely in refrigerator. Serve over ham. Makes 3 cups.
Mrs. Lewis D. Anderson *Mobile, Alabama*

TANGY BARBECUE SAUCE

"Make ahead – refrigerate."

¼ cup Wesson oil
½ cup onion, finely chopped
¾ cup catsup
¾ cup water
⅓ cup fresh lemon juice
3 tablespoons prepared mustard
3 tablespoons sugar
2 teaspoons salt
3 tablespoons Worcestershire sauce
¼ teaspoon black pepper
Tabasco to taste

In medium skillet, brown onions slowly in ¼ cup of oil. Add remaining ingredients. Simmer 30 minutes.
George Robertson, Jr. *Gold Hill, Alabama*

BLENDER BEARNAISE SAUCE

"Excellent on fresh asparagus, steak and poached fish."

2 tablespoons white wine
1 tablespoon tarragon vinegar
2 teaspoons tarragon, chopped
2 teaspoons shallots, chopped
¼ teaspoon freshly ground black pepper
½ cup butter
3 egg yolks
2 tablespoons lemon juice
¼ teaspoon salt
Pinch cayenne pepper

Combine wine, vinegar, tarragon, shallots and pepper in a skillet. Bring to a boil and cook rapidly until almost all the liquid disappears. Heat butter in another saucepan until bubbling but not brown. Place egg yolks, lemon juice, salt and cayenne in electric blender. Cover container and turn motor on and off at high speed. Remove cover; turn the motor on high and gradually add hot butter. (Stop here and it's Hollandaise.) Add herb mixture, cover and blend on high speed 4 seconds.
Mrs. Alton B. James *Mobile, Alabama*

SHRIMP COCKTAIL SAUCE

2 tablespoons horseradish
1 cup catsup
1 teaspoon salt
½ cup lemon juice
2 teaspoons Worcestershire sauce
½ cup celery, finely cut
2 to 3 drops Tabasco

Combine all ingredients
Mrs. Richard F. Bliss (Billie)

LAMB ROAST SAUCE

"Fantastic on grilled lamb chops."

⅓ cup catsup
⅓ cup Worcestershire sauce
⅓ cup water
1 tablespoon sugar
¼ teaspoon salt
Juice of 1 lemon

Put all ingredients in saucepan. Heat to low boil; then simmer. Serve over lamb. Makes 1¼ cups.
Mrs. Michael Reeves (Susan)

REMOULADE SAUCE

1 cup mayonnaise
2 teaspoons parsley, chopped
½ teaspoon dry mustard
1 tablespoon wine vinegar
Juice of 1 lemon
2 tablespoons dry sherry
1 medium onion, grated
Salt and pepper to taste

Combine all ingredients and mix well. Chill until ready to serve over shrimp and lettuce. Use as a salad or appetizer.
Mrs. Ralph E. Gaines, Jr. (Mary Sue)

sea food

SHRIMP, MUSHROOM AND ARTICHOKE CASSEROLE

"Better if made a day ahead."

3 tablespoons butter
½ pound mushrooms
1½ pounds shrimp
1 14-ounce can artichoke hearts
4½ tablespoons butter
4½ tablespoons flour
¾ cup milk
¾ cup whipping cream
½ cup dry sherry
1 tablespoon Worcestershire
Salt and pepper to taste
½ cup Parmesan cheese
Paprika

Melt 3 tablespoons butter and sauté mushrooms; set aside. Boil and shell shrimp. In a 2-quart casserole, layer artichokes, shrimp and mushrooms. In separate saucepan, melt 4½ tablespoons butter. Stirring with a wire whisk, add 4½ tablespoons flour, then the milk and cream. Stir until thickened. Add sherry, Worcestershire, salt and pepper to cream sauce. Pour sauce over layers. Sprinkle top with cheese then sprinkle with paprika. Bake for 20-30 minutes at 375 degrees. Serve over rice. Better if made a day ahead. Serves 6.
Mrs. James W. Heacock, Jr. (Harriet)

SEAFOOD CASSEROLE FOR A CROWD

"Excellent for a crowd."

1 green pepper, chopped
2 stalks celery, chopped
1 medium onion, chopped
2 cups water
1 4-ounce can pimientoes, chopped
3 pounds cooked, deveined shrimp
2 7-ounce cans crabmeat
4 hard cooked eggs, cut up
1½ cups buttered bread crumbs

Combine chopped pepper, celery, onion, and water. Cook until vegetables are tender. Drain. Add pimientoes, shrimp, crabmeat and eggs. Add sauce to shrimp mixture and put in a 3-quart buttered casserole dish. Sprinkle crumbs over top and bake at 400 degrees for 25-30 minutes. Serves 12-15.

Sauce:

4 tablespoons butter
4 tablespoons flour
2 cups light cream
1 cup sharp Cheddar cheese, shredded
Salt and pepper to taste

Melt butter and stir in flour until smooth. Gradually add cream and stir until mixture thickens, stirring constantly. Add cheese, salt and pepper.
Mrs. Jimmy Barnett (Lynn)

SEAFOOD CASSEROLE I

"May be made in advance and refrigerated."

1 cup shrimp, boiled
1 cup oysters or crab meat
1 cup English peas, cooked
½ teaspoon salt
⅛ teaspoon pepper
5 tablespoons onion, chopped
1 green pepper, chopped
1 cup celery, chopped
1½ cups brown rice, cooked
1 teaspoon Worcestershire sauce
1½ cups mayonnaise
Whole wheat bread crumbs

Combine all ingredients except bread crumbs. Pour in buttered 2-quart casserole. Top with bread crumbs. Bake for 30 minutes at 350 degrees. Serves 6.
Mrs. Carson Baker (Sadie)

SEAFOOD CASSEROLE II

"Real guest pleaser."

1 pound shrimp, cooked and shelled
1 7½-ounce can crab meat
1 can water chestnuts, drained and sliced
2 tablespoons butter or oleo
3 tablespoons onion, finely chopped
¼ cup green pepper, finely chopped
2 tablespoons butter or oleo
2 tablespoons all-purpose flour
1 teaspoon salt
½ cup dry sherry
3 cups light cream
1 can French fried onions
1 cup English peas
1 8-ounce package egg noodles, cooked and drained

Combine shrimp, crab and water chestnuts in a large mixing bowl. Heat 2 tablespoons butter in medium saucepan and add onion and green pepper. Sauté 5 minutes or until tender. Add vegetables to seafood mixture. Melt 2 tablespoons butter in same saucepan; stir in flour and salt. Cook 1 minute. Remove pan from heat; stir in sherry and cream gradually. Cook over medium heat, stirring constantly until sauce thickens slightly and comes to a boil. Add to vegetable-seafood mixture. Add ½ can onions and 1 cup peas. Stir in noodles. Spoon into lightly buttered large (3 to 4-quart) baking dish. Bake at 400 degrees for 20 minutes or until bubbly. Remove from oven and sprinkle top with remaining onions. Bake 5 minutes longer.

Mrs. Tony McKinney (Jeanne)

SEAFOOD QUICHE

"May be baked the day before – then warmed."

2 9-inch frozen pie shells
6-ounces king crab, frozen or canned
1½ cups shrimp, peeled, deveined and cooked
8-ounces natural Swiss cheese, chopped
½ cup celery, finely chopped
½ cup onion, finely chopped
4 eggs, slightly beaten
1 cup dry white wine
1 cup mayonnaise
2 tablespoons flour

Combine crab, shrimp, cheese, celery and onion. Pour equally into pie shells. Mix eggs, mayonnaise, wine and flour. Pour equally over crab mixture. Bake at 350 degrees for 45-50 minutes.

Mrs. Jack Edmiston (Candy)

CURRIED SHRIMP IN AVOCADO HALVES

2 avocados
Lime juice
1 tablespoon butter
1 teaspoon curry powder
1 teaspoon salt
⅓ cup onion, chopped
1 large tomato or 1 cup tomatoes, chopped
1½ cups shrimp, cooked
1 cup sour cream
2 cups rice, cooked

Brush avocado halves with lime juice. Place in shallow pan. Heat 10 minutes in 300 degree oven. In saucepan, combine butter, curry powder, salt, tomato and onion. Cook until onion is tender. Add shrimp and heat. Blend in sour cream. Place avocado on top of bed of rice on warm plates and fill halves with curried shrimp. Serves 4.
Mrs. T. E. Christenberry (Frankie)

FRIED SHRIMP WITH BEER BATTER

"Very tasty."

1 pound raw shrimp, shelled and deveined
1 tablespoon cognac or rum
1 teaspoon Worcestershire sauce
Fat for deep frying
Frying batter (see below)
Mayonnaise and capers

Marinate shrimp in cognac and Worcestershire sauce about 30 minutes. Dip a few shrimp at a time in the batter and fry in deep, hot oil until golden brown. Drain on absorbent paper. Serve with mayonnaise seasoned with capers. Serves 3.

Frying batter:

½ cup flour
Pinch of salt
1 tablespoon melted butter
1 egg, beaten
½ cup beer
1 egg white, stiffly beaten

Sift flour and salt into mixing bowl. Stir in butter and egg. Add beer gradually, stirring only until mixture is smooth. Let batter stand in warm place for one hour; then, fold in beaten egg white.
Mrs. Bob Burton Birmingham, Alabama

SHRIMP AND WILD RICE SUPREME

"A crowd pleaser."

2 6-ounce packages Uncle Ben's Wild Rice mixture
2 tablespoons butter
1 cup celery, bias cut
1 5-ounce can mushrooms, sliced and drained
½ cup green onions, sliced
2 tablespoons pimiento, chopped
2 cups shrimp, cooked (Reserve 6 to 8 for garnish)
⅛ to ¼ teaspoon pepper

Cook rice according to directions. In a large skillet sauté celery and mushrooms in butter until crispy tender. Stir in onions, pimiento and shrimp. Turn rice into skillet and blend ingredients carefully. Put into a 2 quart baking dish.

Topping:

1 10½-ounce can mushroom soup
1½ cups sour cream
2 tablespoons butter
⅔ cup bread crumbs
2 tablespoons parsley, chopped

Combine soup and sour cream. Mix well. Spoon over shrimp and rice mixture. Toss bread crumbs with melted butter. Add parsley and sprinkle over soup. Bake at 325 degrees for 30 minutes. Top with remaining shrimp and bake 5-10 minutes. Freezes well. Serves 8-10.

Mrs. Robert T. Mallis   Dunwoody, Georgia

SHRIMP SALAD SANDWICHES

1 cup shrimp, cooked and chopped (fresh or canned)
1 3-ounce package cream cheese, softened
2 tablespoons mayonnaise
1 tablespoon catsup
1 teaspoon prepared mustard
Dash of garlic powder
¼ cup celery, finely chopped
1 teaspoon onion, finely chopped (optional)

Mix ingredients thoroughly. Use for making sandwiches, stuffing tomatoes or serving on lettuce. Serves 4.

Mrs. Gordon Herring (Maxine)

SEAFOOD STUFFED EGGPLANT

6 medium eggplant
Bread crumbs
Slivered almonds
Cheddar cheese, grated

Stuffing:

1 teaspoon salt
2 cups onion, minced
2 cups celery, diced
½ teaspoon Accent
3 tablespoons parsley, minced
½ teaspoon nutmeg
8 tablespoons pimiento, chopped
1 cup thick white sauce
3 cups Chinese vegetables, drained
1 teaspoon soy sauce
2 cloves garlic, crushed
¼ cup chili sauce
48 raw shrimp
24 raw scallops
½ pound crabmeat
½ cup mushrooms, drained

Thick White Sauce:

¼ cup butter
¼ cup flour
¼ teaspoon salt
⅛ teaspoon pepper
1 cup milk

Halve eggplants lengthwise. Scoop out pulp; dice and steam until partially cooked. Make white sauce by melting butter in saucepan and blending in flour, salt and pepper. Cook over low heat and gradually stir in milk. Boil and stir 1 minute stirring constantly. Mix eggplant with stuffing ingredients. Fill eggplant shells. Top with bread crumbs and almonds. Put shells in buttered shallow 3-quart baking dish. Bake ½ hour at 350 degrees. Top with cheese just before removing from oven. Serves 12.
Mrs. Nauburn Finis Jones (Margaret)

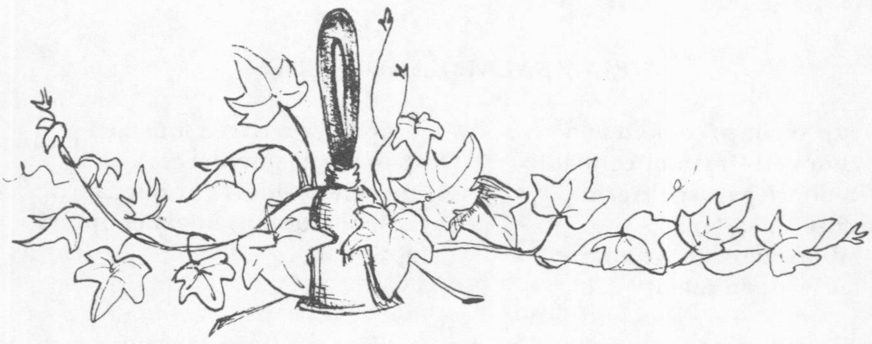

MINCED OYSTERS

½ medium onion, chopped
1 cup celery, chopped
1 stick butter
1 quart oysters, cut into pieces
1 pint toasted biscuit crumbs
4 eggs, well beaten
Juice of ½ lemon
Salt, pepper, Worcestershire sauce to taste

Sauté onion and celery in butter. Combine other ingredients, mixing well. Add to onion and celery and cook until thick. Place on oyster shells, covering lightly with additional bread crumbs and bits of butter. Brown in oven.
Mrs. L. J. Evans (Thelma)

SHRIMP MADRAS

"A super flavor."

2 pounds fresh shrimp
½ teaspoon dried mint flakes
¼ teaspoon dried red pepper flakes
2 to 2½ teaspoons turmeric
½ teaspoon ground coriander
Salt and pepper
1 teaspoon grated ginger or half the amount powdered
2 cloves garlic, minced
½ teaspoon ground cumin
1 medium onion, grated
4 tablespoons butter
1 cup yogurt
1 teaspoon liquid from chutney
2 tablespoons parsley, chopped
Juice of half of a lemon

Peel shrimp and clean. Place in large bowl and add mint, red pepper, tumeric, coriander, salt and pepper to taste, ginger, garlic and cumin. Mix well with hands and let stand an hour or so in refrigerator. Peel and grate onion. Heat 3 tablespoons butter in deep skillet and add onion. Cook until tender. Add remaining butter and shrimp mixture. Cook, gently stirring shrimp, until shrimp turns red all over. Add yogurt and chutney liquid. Simmer 10 minutes covered. Uncover and cook over moderately high heat 10 minutes longer. Add parsley, lemon juice, and salt and pepper to taste. Serve with rice and appropriate condiments: banana, chutney, peanuts, hard boiled eggs, pecans, chopped bacon, coconut and raisins. Serves 4-5.
Mrs. Alton James Mobile, Alabama

SHRIMP VICTORIA

"Gets rave reviews from everyone."

1½ pounds raw shrimp
3 tablespoons shallots, minced
6 tablespoons margarine
¾ pound fresh mushrooms
1½ tablespoons all-purpose flour
¾ teaspoon salt
¾ teaspoon pepper
4½ tablespoons sherry
2¼ cups sour cream
Wild or regular rice

Shell and clean the shrimp and sauté them along with the minced shallots in the margarine until shrimp are pink. Add the mushrooms and cook for 5 minutes adding another tablespoon margarine, if needed. Sprinkle with flour, salt and pepper. Add sherry and sour cream. Cook gently until hot and serve with cooked rice. Serves 8.

Mrs. Gary Heacock   Griffin, Georgia

SHRIMP CREOLE

"Real company fare."

1½ cups onion, chopped
1 cup celery, finely chopped
2 medium green peppers, chopped
2 cloves garlic, minced
¼ cup butter or margarine
1 15-ounce can tomato sauce
1 cup water
2 teaspoons snipped parsley
1 teaspoon salt
⅛ teaspoon cayenne red pepper
2 bay leaves, crushed
14 to 16 ounces cleaned raw shrimp, fresh or frozen
3 cups rice, cooked

Sauté onion, celery, green pepper and garlic in butter until onion is tender. Remove from heat; stir in tomato sauce, water and seasonings. Simmer uncovered for 10 minutes. (Add water if needed.) Stir in shrimp; heat to boiling. Cover and cook over medium heat 10-20 minutes. Serve over rice. Serves 6.

Mrs. Will Lawrence (Sally)
Similar recipe submitted by Mrs. Richard F. Bliss (Billie)

RUFUS'S OYSTER CASSEROLE

"You'll find this a delight."

1 pint oysters
2 tablespoons butter
1 heaping tablespoon flour
Ritz crackers, whole (1 section in 3 part box)
Salt and pepper
2 cups milk, approximately

Melt butter in double boiler. Add flour, salt and pepper. Gradually add milk and cook slowly until sauce thickens. Butter 1½-quart glass baking dish. Place layer of crackers on bottom. Make a layer of oysters. Repeat until all oysters are used; end with layer of crackers. Pour sauce over the crackers and oysters. Bake at 350 degrees approximately 30 minutes or until bubbly and browned. Same sauce may be used for asparagus or broccoli casseroles. Serves 4.

Mrs. Otis R. Burton, Jr. (Louise)

SALMON ROLL

"An original recipe."

Pie crust dough (enough for 2 shells)
1 15½-ounce can Argo salmon
1 cup mayonnaise
1 cup sharp Cheddar, grated
3 cups medium cream sauce
1 cup celery, chopped
¼ cup bell pepper, chopped
½ cup onion, chopped
1 4½-ounce can tiny English peas
2 boiled eggs, chopped

Roll dough out into a thin rectangle. Mince salmon, add mayonnaise and cheese. Mix and spread over dough; then roll jelly roll fashion. Place on baking sheet, split side down. Prick with fork, brush with milk, and bake at 375 degrees for 35 minutes. Make a medium cream sauce. Sauté celery, bell pepper, and onion; add to cream sauce. Add peas and eggs to cream sauce. Cut roll in diagonal pieces and serve with hot cream sauce. Serves 8-10.

Mrs. W. T. Jenkins (Pauline)

GRILLED FISH FILET

"Try this on your grill."

Mackerel or Red Snapper Filet
1 strip of bacon
1 slice of onion
1 slice of lemon

Place fish on buttered aluminum foil. Layer bacon, onion, and lemon on filet. Stick a toothpick through all to hold in place. Fold foil up around sides to make a tray. On gas grill, cook 25 minutes on medium heat with lid down. On charcoal grill, make a hood over fish using extra foil. Cook same as gas grill.
Mrs. Wallis Elliott (Dede)

DEVILED CRAB

"Should be made in advance."

2 small white onions, finely chopped
½ small green pepper, finely chopped
1 teaspoon butter
1 cup mushrooms, chopped (fresh or canned)
Dash of parsley, chopped
Dash of cayenne pepper
Salt to taste
½ teaspoon nutmeg
1 pound flaked crab meat
2 egg yolks
¼ cup buttered bread crumbs
Paprika

White Sauce:

2 tablespoons flour
2 tablespoons butter
1 cup milk

Sauté onion and pepper in butter until soft (not brown). Add mushrooms and continue to sauté for 10 minutes. Add spices. Remove shell from crab meat and add to mixture. Add egg yolks. In separate saucepan, melt 2 tablespoons butter. Blend in flour; add milk and cook over medium heat until thickened. Add this to first mixture. Place in greased crab shells or casserole dish. Cover with buttered bread crumbs and dash with paprika. Store in refrigerator from 4-12 hours before baking. Place shells in shallow pan containing 1 inch of water. Bake 15 minutes at 350 degrees. Freezes well. Serves 8.
Mrs. Lyle Shepler Montgomery, Alabama

CRAB MEAT CROQUETTES

3 tablespoons butter
½ cup onion, grated
3 tablespoons flour
1 cup milk
¼ teaspoon pepper
½ teaspoon salt
1 teaspoon Worcestershire
2 cups crab meat
1½ cups cracker meal or crumbs
2 eggs, slightly beaten
1 cup almonds, ground

Melt butter in skillet; add onions and sauté, then drain. Mix flour and milk and add gradually, stirring constantly until mixture thickens. Add seasonings, then mix with crab meat. Chill at least one hour. Form into 1 to 1½-inch balls and roll in cracker crumbs, then egg, then almonds. Fry in deep fat for 3-5 minutes at 375 degrees.

Sauce:

1 cup chili sauce
¼ cup green pepper, chopped
1 teaspoon lemon juice
1 tablespoon Worcestershire
½ pound fresh mushrooms, sliced

While crab meat mixture is chilling, combine all ingredients for sauce and simmer at least 30 minutes. Serve croquettes in sauce. Makes 18 croquettes. Serves 6-8.
Mrs. William B. McGehee (Mary Lib)

BROILED CRAB OPEN-FACERS

"Good for lunch or brunch."

4 English muffins
1 7½-ounce can crab meat, drained and flaked
¼ cup mayonnaise
1 3-ounce package cream cheese, softened
1 egg yolk
1 teaspoon onion, finely chopped
¼ teaspoon prepared mustard
Dash of salt

Split, butter and lightly toast muffins. Mix crab meat and mayonnaise together and set aside. Mix together cream cheese, egg yolk, onion, mustard and salt until smooth and creamy. Spread muffin halves with butter, then with crab mixture. Top with cream cheese mixture. Broil lightly. Serves 4.
Mrs. Bill Perry (Linda)

TUNA A LA STROGANOFF

2 7-ounce cans tuna, drained
1 chicken bouillon cube
1 cup boiling water
½ cup onion, chopped
1 8-ounce can mushrooms, stems and pieces
¼ cup butter or margarine, melted
2 tablespoons flour
2 tablespoons catsup
¼ teaspoon Worcestershire
Dash of pepper
½ cup sour cream
2 cups cooked rice

Drain tuna. Break into large pieces. Dissolve bouillon cube in boiling water. Cook onion and mushrooms in butter until tender. Blend in flour and brown. Add bouillon gradually and cook until thick, stirring constantly. Add remaining ingredients, except rice. Heat. Serve over rice. Serves 6.
Mrs. Gene Caldwell (Nell)

TUNA ORIENTAL SANDWICH

1 7-ounce can tuna
1 8-ounce can water chestnuts, sliced
¼ cup mayonnaise
1 tablespoon minced onion
1 teaspoon lemon juice
1 teaspoon soy sauce
½ teaspoon curry powder
6 slices of white or French bread

Drain tuna and water chestnuts. Combine all ingredients and mix well. Spread on bread slices and broil until hot. Can be prepared in advance and served cold as a salad.
Mrs. Robert Avery (Mary Virginia)

TUNA BURGERS

"Great for Saturday lunch or a table of bridge."

1 7-ounce can tuna, drained
1½ teaspoon prepared mustard
1 teaspoon Worcestershire
¼ cup mayonnaise
1 tablespoon onion, grated
2 tablespoons green pepper, chopped
2 hamburger buns, split
4 tomato slices
½ cup mayonnaise
½ cup cheese, finely shredded

Blend tuna, mustard, Worcestershire, ¼ cup mayonnaise, onion, and pepper. Place ¼ mixture on each bun half. Top with tomato slice. Blend ½ cup mayonnaise with cheese and spread on tomato slices. Broil 4 inches from heat until topping puffs and browns. Rye bread may be used. Serves 4.
Lena Smith Birmingham, Alabama

HOT CROSSED TUNA CASSEROLE

2 7-ounce cans tuna, drained
1 10-ounce package frozen peas, thawed
1 cup Cheddar cheese, shredded
½ cup bread crumbs
1 cup celery, sliced
¼ cup onion, chopped
¼ teaspoon salt
⅛ teaspoon pepper
1 cup salad dressing
1 8-ounce can refrigerated crescent rolls
Sesame seeds (optional)

Combine tuna, peas, cheese, celery, crumbs, onion, seasonings and salad dressing. Mix well. Spoon into 10 x 6-inch baking dish. Separate dough into two rectangles; press perforations to seal. Cut dough into four long and eight short strips. Place strips over casserole in a lattice design. Brush lightly with additional salad dressing; sprinkle with sesame seeds, if desired. Bake at 350 degrees for 35-40 minutes or until crust is golden brown. Serves 6-8.
Mrs. Andy Brown (Sissy)

CRAB MEAT CASSEROLE

"Serve with tossed salad and baked potato."

1 cup milk
1 cup mayonnaise
1 teaspoon Tabasco sauce
1 teaspoon Worcestershire sauce
½ cup celery, chopped
½ cup green pepper, chopped
½ cup onion, chopped
1 teaspoon salt
¼ pound saltines, crumbled
1 pound crab meat or 3 small cans

Mix all ingredients together and pour into casserole dish. May be topped with cracker crumbs and paprika. Bake 40 minutes at 350 degrees.
Mrs. William J. Munroe (Rachel)

Isbell Bank

by Barbara Sweat

Vegetables

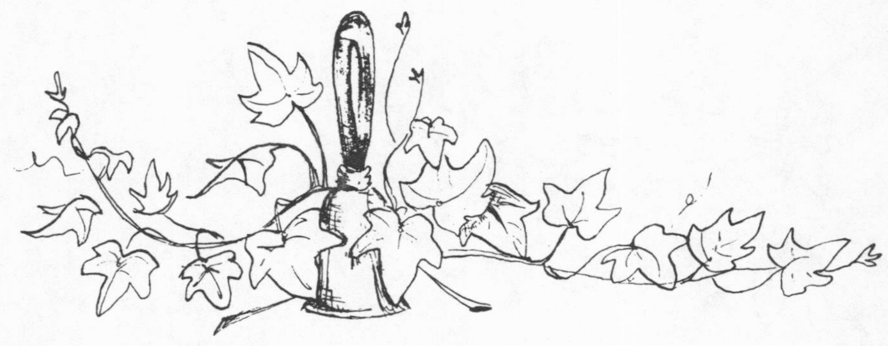

ASPARAGUS RAGOUT

"The nuts make the difference"

1 10½-ounce can asparagus
1 can cream of mushroom soup
1½ cups cracker crumbs
1 cup grated cheese
½ cup salted nuts, crushed
2 tablespoons chopped pimento

Dilute soup with asparagus liquid. Arrange layers of cracker crumbs, asparagus, nuts, and soup, reserving half of each ingredient. Repeat the layers. Cover with grated cheese and dot with pimento. Bake at 350 degrees until cheese is bubbly. Serves 6.
Mrs. A. O. Yoe (Marian)
Similar recipe submitted by Mrs. Jake Pate (Virginia)

ASPARAGUS-PEA CASSEROLE

3 tablespoons butter
3 tablespoons flour
1 cup milk
1 10½-ounce can asparagus, drained
1 8½-ounce can LeSueur peas, drained
1 boiled egg, chopped
½ cup grated cheese
6 crackers (Ritz or Saltine)

Melt butter in a small saucepan. Stir in flour one tablespoon at a time. Add milk and stir, cooking on low heat until thick. In a buttered 1½-quart casserole, place alternate layers of drained asparagus and peas with cheese, sauce, and chopped boiled egg. Crumble crackers over top. Heat 20 minutes at 400 degrees. Serve 6.
Mrs. O. Stanley Thornton (Cathy)
Similar recipe submitted by Mrs. Gordon Herring (Maxine)

BEANS IN A BUNDLE

"Eye-appealing dish."

1 can vertical packed whole green beans
Bacon strips
1 2-ounce jar pimento strips
1 8-ounce bottle French dressing

Wrap 8-12 beans in ½ strip of bacon. Place in a pyrex dish, pour French dressing over beans, and marinate overnight. Bake in same pan 25 minutes at 350 degrees or until bacon is done. Garnish with pimento strips. Serves 4.
Mrs. Harry G. Moore, Jr. *Signal Mountain, Tennessee*

GREEN BEANS HORSERADISH

"Pleases both the ladies and the gentlemen."

2 pounds fresh green beans
1 large onion, sliced
Several bits of ham, bacon or salted meat

Wash and snap beans, add onion and meat. Cover with water and cook about three hours or until dark and soft.

Sauce:

1 cup mayonnaise
2 eggs, boiled and chopped
1 teaspoon Worcestershire sauce
1 heaping tablespoon horseradish
Salt and pepper to taste
Garlic salt
Celery salt
Onion salt
1½ teaspoons minced parsley
Juice of one lemon

Have all ingredients at room temperature. Blend sauce ingredients well, adding garlic, celery, and onion salts to taste. This sauce can either be poured over drained beans before serving or served separately to be spooned over individual servings. These are different and go with any meat. Very good cold. Serves 8.
Mrs. W. B. McGehee, III (Evelyn)

GREEN BEAN CASSEROLE

2 tablespoons butter
2 tablespoons flour
1 cup milk
1 16-ounce can French style green beans with almonds
1 small onion, minced
1 tablespoon Worcestershire sauce
½ teaspoon prepared mustard
½ cup ripe olives, sliced
1 3½-ounce can fried onion rings

Melt butter. Stir in flour. Gradually add milk, stirring constantly, until sauce is thick. Stir in drained green beans, onion, Worcestershire sauce, mustard, and ripe olives. Place in casserole dish and top with onion rings. Bake at 350 degrees for 35 - 45 minutes. This casserole can be made ahead, adding topping just prior to baking. One cup of coarsely crushed potato chips may be substituted for onion rings. Serves 6.
Mrs. Lyle Shepler *Montgomery, Alabama*

COMPANY BEANS

"Some like it hot . . . some like it cold."

2 9-ounce packages frozen French cut green beans
2 9-ounce packages frozen baby lima beans
2 9-ounce packages frozen English peas

Cook vegetables according to directions on packages. Drain liquid; place hot vegetables in serving dish.

Sauce: Ingredients should be at room temperature.

2 cups mayonnaise
1 tablespoon Worcestershire sauce
2 tablespoons vegetable oil
1 medium size onion, minced
4 eggs, boiled and minced
Salt and pepper to taste

Mix this sauce and pour over hot vegetables. This is very good for a buffet dinner and is good leftover as a cold salad. Do not reheat. Canned vegetables can be used. Serves 20-24.
Mrs. John D. Hill (Jeannie)
Mrs. John A. Quenelle *Sylacauga, Alabama*

GRAMMA'S BAKED BEANS

"Twas the night before the picnic . . ."

1½ pounds great Northern beans
1 teaspoon dry mustard
¾ cup brown sugar
2 tablespoons molasses
1 pound lean salt pork
Water

Soak beans overnight. Mix drained beans, mustard, sugar and molasses. Score rind of salt pork. Place half of the salt pork on the bottom of bean pot. Pour in bean mixture. Place remaining pork on top of beans and cover with water. Cook at 300 degrees for 10-12 hours. Water must be added at intervals to keep beans moist. Serves 8-10.
Mrs. Ray Miller (Marianne)

BAKED BEAN CASSEROLE

"Quick and easy for before the home games."

1 pound ground beef
1 small onion, chopped
1 small bell pepper, chopped
½ cup catsup
1 teaspon mustard
¼ cup brown sugar, packed
1 16-ounce can pork and beans
¼ cup water

Brown ground beef and drain well. Add onion and pepper; cook until they are tender but not brown. Remove from heat. Stir in remaining ingredients. Pour into casserole and bake at 400 degrees for 30 minutes. This reheats well. Serves 6.
Mrs. Carl R. Reaves (Joyce)

RED BEANS AND RICE

"Toss a salad and you've got it made."

2 15-ounce cans red kidney beans
1 medium onion, chopped
1 bell pepper, chopped
¼ teaspoon Tabasco
2 teaspoons Worcestershire sauce
1 15-ounce can stewed tomatoes
1 tablespoon cornstarch
1 cup water
1 cup uncooked rice
2½ cups water, salted
Salt and pepper to taste

In a 2-quart saucepan, cook first six ingredients until the pepper and onion are tender. Add the cornstarch to the water and stir into bean mixture. Add salt and pepper. Cook until thickened. Cook rice in salted water while bean mixture cooks. Serve red beans over rice. This can be made ahead and warmed up. Serves 4.
Mrs. Cleve Jacobs (Patti)

RED BEANS AND RICE

4 cans New Orleans style kidney beans
1 pound ground chuck
1 large onion, chopped
1 small clove garlic, minced
1 cup ham, diced

Mash two cans of beans in a bowl and set aside. Brown ground chuck, onion, garlic and diced ham in a large skillet. Add mashed beans and simmer ten minutes. Put whole beans and meat mixture together in a large pot and cook slowly for one hour. Serve over rice with a salad and French bread.
Mrs. Charles Osborne (wife of Charles Osborne, Mayor of Talladega)

COUNTRY BAKED BEANS

"An absolute necessity with barbecue."

4 pieces bacon, fried and drained
1 1-pound 15-ounce can pork and beans, drained
1 16-ounce can kidney beans, drained
1 8-ounce can lima beans, drained
1 small bell pepper, chopped (optional)
1 medium onion, chopped
2 tablespoons bacon drippings
¾ cup brown sugar
1 tablespoon mustard
3 tablespoons Worcestershire sauce
⅓ cup catsup
¼ teaspoon pepper
Salt to taste

Fry bacon and crumble. Mix all beans and chopped bell pepper and place in a 2½-3-quart casserole dish. Brown onion in bacon drippings. To browned onion, add remaining ingredients and cook over medium heat for 10 minutes. Add cooked mixture and crumbled bacon to beans. Bake, covered, at 350 degrees for 30 minutes. Remove cover and bake an additional 15 minutes. May be prepared a day or two in advance and refrigerated. Serves 16.
Mrs. O. Stanley Thornton (Cathy)

CONTINENTAL VEGETABLE CASSEROLE

"Well worth your time."

1 16-ounce can baby lima beans
1 16-ounce can French-cut green beans
1 16-ounce can English peas
2 tablespoons margarine
3 tablespoons flour
1¾ cups milk
2 eggs, hard boiled
2 tablespoons lemon juice
2 teaspoons dried onion bits
1 teaspoon Worcestershire sauce
1 teaspoon prepared mustard
½ teaspoon garlic salt
1 2-ounce jar sliced pimento
¼ cup slivered almonds
1 cup mayonnaise
8 slices bread
6 tablespoons margarine

Drain vegetables in colander. Melt 2 tablespoons butter in a saucepan. Stir in flour until smooth. Add milk. Cook until smooth and thick, stirring constantly. Add remaining ingredients, except for bread and 6 tablespoons margarine, to sauce mixture and stir in well. Put this mixture in a 13 x 9 x 2-inch baking dish. To prepare bread crumbs, bake bread at 300 degrees for 20 minutes. Place on waxed paper and roll with rolling pin. Melt butter in saucepan and stir into bread crumbs. Sprinkle crumbs over top of casserole. Bake at 350 degrees for 20 minutes. Serves 16-20.
Mrs. Crawford Nelson (Linda)

BEETS IN ORANGE SAUCE

"Best beets ever."

1 tablespoon cornstarch
1 tablespoon sugar
¼ teaspoon salt
¼ cup water
⅔ cup fresh orange juice
1 tablespoon fresh lemon juice
2 tablespoons butter
½ teaspoon grated orange peel
1 16-ounce can sliced beets, drained

Combine cornstarch, sugar, and salt in saucepan; gradually add water, orange and lemon juices, blending well. Cook over low heat, stirring constantly until thickened and clear, 4 to 5 minutes. Add butter, grated peel, and drained beets and simmer until just heated through. Serves 4.
Mrs. James Hardwick (Dot)

BROCCOLI-RICE CASSEROLE

2 10-ounce packages frozen chopped broccoli
1 large onion, chopped
1 stick margarine
1 cup uncooked brown rice
1 can cream of chicken soup
1 can Cheddar cheese soup

Cook broccoli according to directions on package. Drain well. Sauté onion in margarine. Cook rice according to directions. Combine all ingredients with both soups in a buttered casserole dish. Bake at 350 degrees for 25 minutes. Serves 8-10.

Mrs. Robert C. Lumpkin (Beth)
Mrs. Helen Orser   Opelika, Alabama

BROCCOLI SOUFFLE

2 10-ounce packages frozen chopped broccoli
1 cup mayonnaise
1 can cream of mushroom soup
3 tablespoons onion, grated
3 eggs, well beaten
1 cup sharp Cheddar cheese, grated
¾ cup Ritz cracker crumbs

Cook broccoli according to directions on package; drain and cool. Mix broccoli with remaining ingredients except cracker crumbs and place in a 9 x 12-inch casserole. Sprinkle with cracker crumbs. Cook at 350 degrees for 30 minutes. Can be made ahead. Serves 8.

Mrs. Jack R. Edmiston (Candace)

BROCCOLI WITH SOUR CREAM SAUCE

2 10-ounce packages frozen broccoli
2 tablespoons butter
2 tablespoons onion, minced
1½ cups sour cream
2 teaspoons sugar
1 teaspoon vinegar
½ teaspoon poppy seeds
½ teaspoon paprika
¼ teaspoon salt
Dash of black pepper

Cook broccoli according to directions on package. Drain well. Melt butter in a saucepan and sauté onion. Remove from heat and stir in sour cream, sugar, vinegar, poppy seed, paprika, salt and pepper. Place broccoli on a heated serving platter and pour sauce over. Serves 8.

Miss Martha G. Williams

FRESH BROCCOLI WITH CHEESE-ALMOND SAUCE

"Good and pretty."

1 large bunch fresh broccoli
1 can cream of mushroom soup
¾ cup mayonnaise
1 cup sharp Cheddar cheese, grated
1½ tablespoons lemon juice
½ cup chopped pimento
⅓ cup slivered almonds
¾ cup Nabisco Cheese Nibs, crushed

Wash broccoli and cut into 4 inch lengths. Cook uncovered until just tender in a small amount of salted water. Place broccoli in three rows in a buttered 3-quart casserole dish. Mix the soup, mayonnaise, cheese, and lemon juice; pour down the middle of broccoli rows. Garnish with pimento and almonds. Sprinkle cracker crumbs over top, leaving some of the pimento and other ingredients showing. Bake uncovered at 350 degrees for 20 minutes or until bubbly. Frozen broccoli (3 10-ounce packages) can be substituted, but fresh is better. Serves 6.
Mrs. Phillip Hardy Smith (Catherine)

DEVILED CORN

4 tablespoons butter
2 tablespoons flour
1 teaspoon prepared mustard
½ teaspoon Worcestershire sauce
1 tablespoon lemon juice
½ teaspoon salt
Dash of pepper
½ cup milk
3 slices bacon, cooked and crumbled
2 hard-boiled eggs, chopped
1 16-ounce can whole-kernel corn, drained
1 16-ounce can cream-style corn
½ cup grated Parmesan cheese
½ cup cracker crumbs
1 tablespoon butter, melted

Melt 4 tablespoons butter in pan. Stir in flour, mustard, Worcestershire sauce, lemon juice, salt, and pepper. Add milk. Cook till mixture thickens and bubbles. Remove from heat. Stir in bacon, eggs, and corn. Put in 1½-quart casserole. Sprinkle cheese on top. Combine cracker crumbs and melted butter and sprinkle over cheese. Bake at 350 degrees for 45 minutes or until it bubbles. Can be prepared ahead. Good with pork. Serves 6.
Mrs. James Heacock, Jr. (Harriet)

CORN PUDDING DELUXE

2 cups milk
½ stick margarine, melted
4 slices bread
4 eggs, beaten until fluffy
2 10-ounce packages frozen creamed corn
½ cup sugar
Salt and pepper to taste
1 cup cheese, grated

Combine milk and margarine. Pour over bread slices, soak, break slices into pieces. Mix in eggs. Add this to corn seasoned with sugar, salt and pepper. Bake at 300 degrees for 30 minutes or until slightly browned. Top with grated cheese just as you take it from the oven. Serves 8-10.
Mrs. Larkin Coker (Joan)
Mrs. Pope Wilder (Frances)

SKILLET CABBAGE

"Try it – you'll love it!"

½ medium cabbage
1 medium onion
1 bell pepper
3 stalks celery
1 or 2 tomatoes
1 tablespoon bacon drippings
1 teaspoon salt
¼ teaspoon pepper

Chop the vegetables quite fine. Melt the bacon drippings in a skillet; toss in chopped vegetables. Season with salt and pepper. Mix well, cover and cook over moderate heat, stirring occasionally, for 5-8 minutes or until cabbage is tender-crisp. Serves 4-6.
Misses Toni and Nora Hardiman *Birmingham, Alabama*

CABBAGE CASSEROLE

"Economical and delicious."

1 medium cabbage, shredded
4 tablespoons margarine, melted
4 tablespoons plain flour
½ teaspoon salt
¼ teaspoon pepper
2 cups milk
½ bell pepper, chopped
½ medium onion, chopped
⅔ cup Cheddar cheese, grated
½ cup mayonnaise
3 tablespoons chili sauce

Shred cabbage. Boil in salted water about 15 minutes or until tender. Drain and place in a 13 x 9 x 2-inch baking dish. Combine butter and flour in a small saucepan over low heat. Stir until smooth and bubbly. Add salt, pepper and milk; stir constantly until thick. Pour sauce over cabbage and bake at 375 degrees for 20 minutes. Combine remaining ingredients. Mix well and stir into cabbage mixture. Bake at 400 degrees for 20 minutes. Serves 10-12.

Mrs. James D. Luker, Jr. (Judy)
Mrs. Curtis O'Daniel (Judy)

MARINATED CARROTS

"Just a little something extra."

2 pounds carrots, peeled and sliced
1 onion, thinly sliced
1 small bell pepper, thinly sliced
1 can condensed tomato soup
½ cup vegetable oil
¾ cup cider vinegar
1 cup sugar
1 teaspoon prepared mustard
1 teaspoon Worcestershire sauce
1 teaspoon salt
1 teaspoon pepper

Cook carrots until tender. Drain and cool. Arrange carrots, onion and pepper slices in layers in a deep bowl. Combine remaining ingredients in a blender or heat and stir until well mixed. Cool. Pour over carrots, onions and peppers. Cover and let marinate at least 24 hours in the refrigerator. Will keep a week or more. May be served hot or cold. Serves 15-20.

Mrs. David Beasley (Ellen)
Mrs. Bill Parker (Dorothy)
Mrs. C. Woodrow Stone *Baxley, Georgia*

ONION PIE

"Delicious with cold cuts and coffee."

4 slices bacon, fried
2½ pounds white onions, chopped
½ bell pepper, chopped
2 stems parsley, chopped
3 tablespoons butter
4 tablespoons flour
3 to 4 dashes hot sauce
¼ teaspoon salt
1 teaspoon Worcestershire sauce
1½ 5-ounce cans Pet milk
6-7 tablespoons water
5 eggs, beaten
2 9-inch frozen deep dish pie crusts
Parmesan cheese

Fry bacon crisp, remove and crumble. To bacon drippings, add onions, pepper, parsley, and butter; cook well, stirring for 10 minutes. Add flour, hot sauce, salt, Worcestershire sauce, ½ can Pet milk, and water, stir well and let set without heat. Beat eggs and add one can Pet milk to eggs. Gradually add onion mixture until all is added. Pour into pie crusts. Sprinkle tops with bacon and Parmesan cheese. Place on cookie sheet and bake for 30-35 minutes at 350 degrees. Each pie serves 8.
Mrs. L. M. Stone (Lettie)
Similar recipe submitted by Mrs. John Norman (Edith)

CREAMED CELERY

2 cups celery, chopped in ½ inch pieces
2 tablespoons margarine
2 tablespoons plain flour
1 cup chicken broth
¼ cup milk
Salt and pepper to taste
¼ cup almonds, chopped and blanched
½ cup grated Cheddar cheese
½ cup bread crumbs

Parboil celery in a small amount of water until almost tender. Set aside. In a saucepan, melt butter and stir in flour until smooth. Add chicken broth and milk and cook over low heat until thickened. Add celery and almonds to sauce. Pour mixture into a casserole dish and sprinkle with grated cheese and bread crumbs. Bake at 375 degrees for 25-30 minutes. Serves 6.
Mrs. Norman Wood (Madge)

TURKEY OR CHICKEN DRESSING

4 medium onions, chopped
5 stalks celery, finely chopped
⅓ cup bacon drippings
2 cups half stale white bread, crumbled
2 cups eggbread, crumbled
1 tablespoon sugar
Pepper to taste
3 eggs, beaten
Chicken or turkey broth

Fry onions and celery in drippings until almost done. Crumble breads together, add all ingredients including enough broth to make dressing of pouring consistency. Pour into a baking dish about 3 inches deep and bake until well set and brown on top. Serve with giblet gravy. Serves 8.
Purefoy Hotel Cookbook, Compliments of Mrs. Edward Hyde (Dorothy)

DRESSING

4 to 5 slices bread, toasted and crumbled
3 to 4 turkey or chicken bouillon cubes
Turkey broth
1 8½-ounce package Jiffy corn muffin mix, prepared according to directions
¾ cup cornflakes, crushed
1 small onion, chopped
4 eggs, slightly beaten
½ stick margarine
Salt and pepper to taste

Crumble toast and muffins. Dissolve bouillon cubes in 1 cup of broth. Pour over bread crumbs and mash. Add remaining ingredients, mixing well. Then add more broth until dressing is of a creamy texture. Bake at 325 degrees 30-45 minutes until the top is light brown. When the dressing is served, it should be the consistency of soft grits. Serves 8-10.
Mrs. Robert Weaver (Janette)

PINEAPPLE SOUFFLE

"Put it right next to the ham."

1 cup margarine
1 cup sugar
4 egg yolks
1 15-ounce can crushed pineapple, drained
6 slices bread, remove crust and cube
4 egg whites, beaten until frothy

Cream margarine and sugar. Beat one egg yolk at a time and add to margarine and sugar. Add pineapple and fold in bread crumbs and egg whites. Put in ungreased casserole dish. Bake at 350 degrees for 20 minutes. Serves 6.

Mrs. Roy Burton (Mary Evelyn)
Similar recipe submitted by Mrs. Joe Upchurch (Frances)

CURRIED FRUIT

"Perfect with a quiche."

1 16-ounce can peach halves
1 16-ounce can pear halves
1 15-ounce can pineapple chunks
1 6-ounce jar red cherries
¼ cup butter
¼ cup brown sugar
2 teaspoons curry powder

Open and drain all fruits. Place in flat oblong pyrex dish. Melt butter in a saucepan and add brown sugar and curry powder. When blended, spread over fruit. It will not cover all the fruit, so place at intervals over fruit. Bake at 350 degrees for 1 hour. Serves 6-8.

Mrs. George Jones (Alice)

BAKED BANANAS

"Serve as an accompaniment or a light dessert with cream topping."

6 small firm ripe bananas
1 8-ounce can crushed pineapple with juices
¼ cup honey
1 tablespoon lemon juice
2 teaspoons cornstarch
2 tablespoons butter

Peel bananas and place in a single layer baking dish just large enough for the bananas. Combine pineapple and juice with honey, lemon juice and cornstarch in a bowl. Pour over the bananas. Dot with butter. Bake in a 375 degree oven for 20 minutes or until bananas are softened. Can be prepared ahead of time and kept in a cool place.

Mrs. William A. Davis, Jr (Mona)

HOT FRUIT CASSEROLE

"For that special dinner party."

1 29-ounce can sliced peaches
1 29-ounce can pear halves, quartered
1 15-ounce can pineapple chunks
1 29-ounce can pitted plums
1 10-ounce bottle red cherries
1 cup applesauce
¾ cup dark brown sugar
⅓ cup butter, melted
½ cup slivered almonds
2 bananas, sliced

Drain all fruits. Put in large bowl. Add applesauce and ½ cup brown sugar to melted butter. Bring to a boil. Pour over fruit. Refrigerate over night (or 8 hours). Butter a 2-quart casserole. Chop bananas and add to other fruit. Put all in casserole dish and bake at 350 degrees for 45 minutes. Mix remaining ¼ cup sugar with almonds. Sprinkle over fruit. Bake again until bubbly. This is a delicious side dish for brunch, lunch, or dinner. Add whipped cream for a dessert. Serves 10.
Mrs. Stephen Syer (Marion)

EGGPLANT CREOLE

1 pound eggplant
2 tablespoons margarine
½ cup chopped onion
1 stalk celery
1 large tomato, chopped
2 tablespoons flour
1 teaspoon salt
¼ teaspoon pepper
¼ teaspoon sugar
½ cup buttered bread crumbs
¼ cup shredded Cheddar cheese

Peel and cut eggplant. Cook till tender, drain and chop. Melt butter in skillet and sauté onion and celery for 2-3 minutes. Add tomato, sprinkle with flour and stir well; cook an additional 2-3 minutes. Season with salt, pepper, and sugar. Mix eggplant and tomato mixture and spoon into buttered casserole. Combine buttered bread crumbs and shredded cheese and sprinkle over casserole. Bake at 350 degrees for 25-30 minutes. Serves 6.
Mrs. T. E. Christenberry, Jr. (Frankie)
Similar recipe submitted by Mrs. Ralph Gaines (Mary Sue)

CHEESE GRITS SOUFFLE

"The brunch bunch adores this."

4 cups cooked grits
8 tablespoons butter
6 cups Cheddar cheese, grated
¾ cup milk
8 eggs, beaten separately
¾ teaspoon Tabasco sauce
2 teaspoons monosodium glutamate
½ teaspoon salt
¼ teaspoon powdered garlic

Mix butter and cheese with the hot grits until melted. Add remaining ingredients. Pour into a buttered 2-quart casserole and sprinkle with paprika. Bake at 375 degrees for 45-60 minutes. Freezes well but should defrost before cooking. Serves 12.
Mrs. James W. Heacock, Jr. (Harriet)

GARLIC GRITS

1 cup grits
4½ cups water
1 teaspoon salt
½ pound butter
1 roll garlic cheese
½ cup milk
2 eggs
Pinch cayenne pepper
1 cup potato chips, crushed fine

Pour grits slowly into boiling salted water. Cook until done and cool slightly. Melt butter and ¾ of cheese roll and add to grits. Beat eggs and milk, stir into grits along with cayenne pepper. Pour into a buttered 1 quart casserole. Top with remaining cheese and potato chips. Bake at 350 degrees for 45 minutes. Serves 8.
Mrs. Hugh Brown (Katherine)
Similar recipes submitted by:
Mrs. Frank Harwell (Edith)
Mrs. David Beasley (Ellen)

MUSHROOMS GRUYÉRE

"Goes well with candlelight."

1 pound fresh mushrooms, sliced fine
1 tablespoon chopped shallots
5½ tablespoons unsalted butter
Salt and pepper to taste
2 tablespoons Madeira wine or grated nutmeg
¾ cup heavy cream
1 tablespoon chopped parsley
1 baked pie shell
⅔ cup grated Gruyére cheese

Wipe mushrooms and slice. Sauté chopped shallots in 4 tablespoons hot butter; add mushrooms, lemon juice, salt, and pepper. When mushrooms have lost their moisture, add wine and let evaporate completely to retain only the bouquet. Add ¾ cup cream. Cook gently on low heat until cream has reduced. Add parsley. Fill baked pie shell with the mushroom mixture and cover the edge of the crust with foil. Sprinkle with cheese and baste with 1½ tablespoons melted butter. Broil to brown. Serves 8-10.
Mrs. Barry McCrary (Marilyn)

HOMINY AND ALMOND CASSEROLE

1 can cream of mushroom soup
½ cup Pet milk
⅛ teaspoon cayenne pepper
1 teaspoon celery seed
½ teaspoon black pepper
1 teaspoon Worcestershire sauce
1 29-ounce can hominy
1 cup almonds, chopped
1 cup buttered bread crumbs

Mix soup with milk and seasonings. Simmer over low heat until well blended. Drain hominy and place in casserole. Add almonds to soup mixture. Pour over hominy. Cover with bread crumbs. Bake at 350 degrees for 30-40 minutes. Serves 8.
Mrs. DeSoto Burton (Wells)
Mrs. Roy Burton (Mary Evelyn)

CARROT CHEESE RING MOLD

4 tablespoons butter
2 cups carrots, cooked and mashed
2 cups grated mild Cheddar cheese
2 eggs
½ cup milk
Salt and pepper to taste

Add butter to hot carrots. Combine all other ingredients. Mix well and place in well greased ring mold. Set in pan of hot water. Bake at 350 degrees for 40 minutes or until firm. Can be made the day ahead and baked before serving. Serves 6-8.
Mrs. Cecil G. Brown, Jr. *Roanoke, Alabama*

GLAZED ONIONS

3 cups small white onions
½ cup ketchup
⅓ cup honey
1 tablespoon butter

If fresh onion are used, parboil in salted water about 5 minutes. Drain. Put onions in casserole dish. Cover with ketchup and honey and dot with butter. Cover and bake at 375 degrees for 45 minutes. Uncover and bake for an additional 15 minutes. Serves 6.
Mrs. Gene Caldwell (Nell)

POTATO PANCAKES

"Like Grandma used to make!"

2 eggs
2 tablespoons milk
2 tablespoons melted butter
2 tablespoons flour
¾ teaspoon salt
⅛ teaspoon pepper
¼ small onion, chopped
2 cups peeled raw potatoes, diced

Mix all ingredients in blender. Cook just as you would pancakes. Makes about 8 four-inch pancakes.
Mrs. Toby Deese (Ruth Helen)

CRAB-STUFFED BAKED POTATOES

"Real company fare"

4 medium baking potatoes
½ cup light cream
½ cup butter
1 cup sharp Cheddar cheese, grated
¼ cup grated onion
1 teaspoon salt
½ teaspoon pepper
½ teaspoon paprika
1 6½-ounce can crab meat

Scrub potatoes and dry thoroughly. Bake slowly at 325 degrees until done. Cut lengthwise, scoop out most of potato and place in mixing bowl. Add cream, butter, cheese, salt and pepper, mix until blended. Stir in crab meat. Fill potato skins with mixture. Sprinkle with paprika. Reheat in very hot oven for 15 minutes. Serves 8.

Mrs. Will Beard *Guntersville, Alabama*

DRIED BEEF AND POTATOES

"The way to your man's heart."

2 2½-ounce jars dried beef, shredded
1 tablespoon butter
1 13-ounce can evaporated milk
1 8½-ounce can water chestnuts, drained and sliced
½ cup Cheddar cheese, shredded
2 whole green onions, sliced
¼ teaspoon dry mustard
5 hot baked potatoes
2 tablespoons Cheddar cheese, shredded

Cook and stir beef in butter over medium heat until butter is absorbed. Remove from heat; stir in milk. Heat to boiling, stirring constantly. Boil and stir 1 minute. Stir in water chestnuts, cheese, onions and dry mustard. Heat until water chestnuts are hot. Split hot potatoes lengthwise; fluff with fork. Top potatoes with creamed beef mixture; sprinkle with 2 tablespoons cheese. Serves 5.

Mrs. T. C. Copeland (Barbara)

SWEET POTATO SUPREME

3 cups sweet potatoes, cooked and mashed
1 cup sugar
½ teaspoon salt
2 eggs, beaten
¾ stick margarine, melted
½ cup milk
1½ teaspoons vanilla

Mix all ingredients well and pour into a greased 2-quart casserole dish.

Topping:

⅓ cup flour
1 cup brown sugar, packed
1 cup chopped nuts
⅓ stick margarine, melted
Pinch of salt

Mix topping until crumbly. Sprinkle over potato mixture. Bake at 350 degrees for 30 minutes. May be made ahead and refrigerated before oven time. Serves 8-10.
Mrs. Jane H. Parks, Mrs. Walter Burt (Brenda),
Mrs. O. Stanley Thornton (Cathy), Mrs. David Beasley (Ellen
Variation: Add one can coconut to topping. Mrs. Jack Landham (Joan)

SWEET POTATO CASSEROLE

"A must for holiday feasts."

2 cups sweet potatoes, cooked and mashed
1 cup sugar
1 egg
½ cup coconut, grated
1 cup evaporated milk
1 teaspoon vanilla
Pinch of salt

Mix well, put in greased casserole dish, and bake at 350 degrees for 45 minutes.

Glaze:

1 15-ounce can crushed pineapple and juice
1 8-ounce bottle cherries with juice
1 cup sugar
2 tablespoons cornstarch

Cook together until syrupy. Pour over potato mixture and bake for 10 minutes at 350 degrees. Serves 6-8.
Mrs. Robert Burgess (Eloise)

DELICIOUS SCALLOPED POTATOES

2 tablespoons butter or margarine
2 tablespoons flour
2 cups milk
1½ teaspoons salt
⅛ teaspoon pepper
¼ cup chopped onions
3½ cups potatoes, thinly sliced

In saucepan melt butter. Blend in flour. Slowly add milk and cook over low heat stirring constantly until thick. Add salt, pepper and onion. Place half of the potatoes in a greased 10 x 6 x 2-inch casserole dish. Cover with half the sauce. Repeat layers. Bake covered at 350 degrees for 30 minutes. Uncover and bake an additional 30 minutes. Some tidbits that can be put between layers: 3 slices minced crisp bacon, ¼ cup sliced green pepper, ½ cup chopped ham. Garnish with parsley. Serves 6.
Mrs. W. H. Barton (Gladys)
Mrs. William W. Lawrence (Sally)

POTATO CASSEROLE

"This will become a family favorite."

1 2-pound package frozen hash brown potatoes
1 cup onion, chopped
1 can cream of chicken soup
10 ounces sharp Cheddar cheese, grated
1 cup sour cream
½ cup butter, melted
1 teaspoon salt
1 teaspoon pepper
1 can French fried onions

Mix all ingredients except French fried onions. Place mixture in a casserole dish. Top with French fried onions. Bake at 300 degrees for 1 hour.
Mrs. Hardy Conner (Becky)

RICE CASSEROLE

1 cup raw rice
2 cans beef bouillon
1 can mushrooms, drained
1 small onion, chopped
¼ green pepper, chopped
1 tablespoon Worcestershire sauce
1 tablespoon butter

Combine all ingredients in a 1½ quart casserole dish. Cover. Bake at 300 degrees for 1 hour. Serves 8.
Mrs. Pearino Gaither (Mary)

SPINACH-ARTICHOKE CASSEROLE

"An elegant casserole."

3 9-ounce packages frozen spinach
1 small onion, chopped and sautéed
2 tablespoons lemon juice
2 cans cream of mushroom soup
1 cup sour cream
½ cup mayonnaise
2 8½-ounce cans artichoke hearts, drained
Parmesan cheese

Cook spinach according to package directions and drain. Mix spinach with sautéed onions, lemon juice and mushroom soup. Set aside. Mix sour cream and mayonnaise. In a 2-quart casserole dish alternate layers of spinach mixture with mayonnaise and sour cream. After each layer of mayonnaise mixture, add a few artichokes pushing each down into mayonnaise. Sprinkle with cheese. Bake at 350 degrees for 30 minutes. Serves 8-10.
Mrs. James W. Heacock (Becky)

SPINACH LOAF

"Even non-spinach lovers go for this one."

2 8-ounce packages frozen spinach, cooked and drained
2 tablespoons margarine
3 tablespoons flour
1 cup milk
1 cup sharp Cheddar cheese, grated
¼ teaspoon pepper
2 eggs, slightly beaten

Cook and drain spinach. Melt butter in a saucepan. Stir in flour and milk until smooth. Add cheese and pepper. Mix sauce with spinach. Stir in eggs. Pour into buttered casserole dish and bake at 350 degrees for 35-40 minutes. Serves 8.
Mrs. Ralph Bynum (Sibyl)

SAVORY LEMON-LIME RICE

"For your next bridge luncheon."

2 tablespoons butter
½ clove garlic, minced
1 cup rice
1 cup chicken broth or bouillon
1 cup water
½ teaspoon salt
1½ tablespoon chopped parsley
1 tablespoon lemon juice
1 teaspoon lemon rind, grated
1 teaspoon lime rind, grated

Melt butter in saucepan. Add garlic and sauté until golden. Stir in rice, broth, water and salt. Cover; bring quickly to boil over high heat. Reduce heat to warm and let stay on warm until done (about 20 minutes). Add parsley, lemon juice and rinds. Mix lightly with fork. Serves 4-6.
Mrs.Archer King (Lillie)

RICE ORTÉGA

2 cups rice
½ cup onion, chopped
3 tablespoons butter
1 small Jalapeno pepper mashed with fork
1½ cups sour cream
½ cup cottage cheese
½ bay leaf, crumbled
½ pound Longhorn cheese, grated

Cook rice. Sauté onion in butter. In 2-quart casserole dish, combine rice, onion, pepper, sour cream, cottage cheese and bay leaf. Top with grated cheese. Bake at 375 degrees for 25-30 minutes. Serves 10-12.
Mrs. Emma Lee Tibbits

BAKED RICE FLUFF

3 eggs, separated
1 small onion, cut in half
½ cup butter, melted
1 cup Cheddar cheese, cubed
1 cup parsley sprigs
2 cups cooked rice

Heat oven to 350 degrees. Grease a 2-quart casserole. Put egg yolks, onion, butter and cheese into blender container, cover and process at blend until smooth. Add parsley and process only long enough to chop. Pour over the cooked rice and mix thoroughly. Beat egg whites with rotary beater until stiff, and fold into rice mixture. Bake in prepared casserole for 25 minutes. Serves 8.
Mrs. Ed Hyde, Sr. (Dot)

BAKED ZUCCHINI SQUASH

"That good old pizza flavor."

3 cups zucchini squash, sliced or diced
1 large onion, chopped
1 16-ounce can tomatoes
2 ounces sharp Cheddar cheese, chopped
2 tablespoons oregano
¼ teaspoon garlic salt
¼ teaspoon pepper
2 tablespoons bread crumbs

Spread half of zucchini in bottom of casserole dish. Combine onions and tomatoes and pour half of this mixture over zucchini. Mix cheese, seasonings, and bread crumbs and sprinkle half over tomatoes and onions. Repeat layers. Bake in a preheated 350 degree oven for 25 to 30 minutes or until top is well browned. This can be prepared in advance and refrigerated until time to bake. Serves 6-8.
Mrs. Mary Virginia Avery

CORN, CHEESE, AND TOMATO CASSEROLE

3 slices bread
1 16-ounce can tomatoes, drained
1 16-ounce can shoe peg or yellow niblet corn, drained
¼ cup margarine, melted
1 teaspoon seasoned salt
1 cup grated Cheddar cheese

Place bread on cookie sheet and cook in low oven until crisp (about 30 minutes). Cut in cubes and mix with tomatoes, corn, butter, salt, and ⅔ cup cheese. Pour into shallow 1-quart baking dish and sprinkle with remaining cheese. Bake for 25 minutes at 350 degrees. Can use prepackaged croutons, rather than making them. Serves 8-10.
Mrs. Warren Crow, III *Birmingham, Alabama*

ESCALLOPED TOMATOES

"Exceptionally delicious."

1 small onion, minced
¼ cup butter
½ cup brown sugar
1¼ cup dry bread cubes
1 28-ounce can tomatoes
1 teaspoon salt
⅛ teaspoon pepper
½ teaspoon basil

Sauté minced onions in butter in a heavy skillet. Add brown sugar, stir until melted, then add bread crumbs. Simmer for about 5 minutes. Stir in tomatoes and seasonings. Place in a shallow greased baking dish. Bake at 325 degrees for 45 minutes. The order in which ingredients are added is very important. Serves 4-6.
Mrs. William Davis (Mona)

STUFFED TOMATOES WITH RICE

6 large tomatoes
1½ cups cooked rice
¼ pound sharp Cheddar cheese, grated
1 teaspoon Worcestershire sauce
1 tablespoon chopped parsley
2 tablespoons margarine, melted
Salt to taste

Cut a thin slice from the stem end of the tomato. Scoop out pulp, leaving ¼ inch walls. Turn upside down to drain. Toss remaining ingredients lightly and fill tomatoes with this mixture. Bake at 350 degrees for 15 minutes. Serves 6.
Mrs. Larkin Coker (Joan)

BAKED YELLOW SQUASH WITH FRESH TOMATOES

2 pounds yellow squash
3 medium tomatoes, peeled and sliced
2 small onions, sliced paper thin
1½ teaspoons salt
Fresh ground pepper
3½ tablespoons margarine
Cheddar or Parmesan cheese (optional)

Wash squash and slice. Layer squash in greased 2-quart casserole dish, add layer of tomato slices, then onions. Sprinkle with half the salt and pepper. Repeat until all vegetables are used. Dot with margarine. Cover. Bake at 350 degrees for 45-50 minutes. If desired, sprinkle with cheese. Serves 8.
Mrs. Crook Nicholls (Sue)

SQUASH ROLLS

"Squash for a change."

1¼ pounds yellow squash
½ cup onion, chopped
½ teaspoon sugar
1½ teaspoons salt
1 teaspoon black pepper (optional)
2 eggs, beaten
1 cup Saltine cracker crumbs
Corn meal
Deep fat for frying

Cook squash and onion just until tender. Drain well. Mash; add sugar, salt, pepper, beaten eggs and cracker crumbs. Mix well. Let mixture chill over night. Just before time to serve prepare hot fat. Spoon out squash mixture into three inch rolls and lightly roll in corn meal. Fry until brown on both sides. Serve hot. Serves 10-12.

Mrs. James E. Preuitt (Rona)
Similar recipe submitted by Mrs. Lonnie Clevenger (Mary Burk)

SQUASH CASSEROLE

"Superb."

1 stick margarine
1 package Pepperidge Farm Herb Seasoned stuffing
1½-2 pounds yellow squash cooked, seasoned and mashed
2 medium onions, chopped fine
1 can cream of chicken soup
1 cup sour cream
1 small jar chopped pimento
1 can water chestnuts, sliced

Melt margarine and pour over the stuffing and stir. Line an oblong 2½-quart casserole dish with half of this mixture. Set aside remaining mixture for topping. Mix other ingredients and pour over the stuffing. Sprinkle remaining stuffing mixture on top. Bake at 350 degrees for 30 minutes. Serves 6-8.

Mrs. Hugh Brown (Catherine)
Mrs. Eugene Landreth (Reba)
Mrs. Hugo Molliston (Marion)
Mrs. Stephen F. Syer (Marion)

SOMETHING GOOD SAUCE

"Good with fresh vegetables, turnips and dried beans."

1 16-ounce can sauerkraut, drained
1 medium bell pepper, chopped
1 cup onion, chopped
1 cup celery, chopped
1 2-ounce jar pimiento, chopped
1 cup sugar
⅓ cup vinegar

Mix sauerkraut with all the chopped ingredients. Heat sugar and vinegar in a saucepan; pour over other ingredients that have been put in a jar for storage in the refrigerator. This mixture will keep for several weeks if kept in the refrigerator. Makes 1½ quarts.
Mrs. Joe Woodard (Jerry)

Covered Bridge at Waldo
by Marian Yoe

Salads

salads

AVOCADO-CELERY TOMATOES

"A great combination."

3 large avocados, cubed
1 cup celery, diced
1 tablespoon onion, minced
3 tablespoons olive oil
1 tablespoon lemon juice
1 tablespoon mayonnaise
1 tablespoon parsley, minced
⅛ teaspoon cayenne pepper
8 tomatoes

Combine avocados, celery, onion and olive oil; toss well. Add remaining ingredients except tomatoes. Stuff in peeled tomatoes and chill well. For a luncheon entrée, add crabmeat or shrimp to the avocados. Serves 8.
Mrs. Thomas B. Richardson, Jr. (Elaine)

SAUERKRAUT SALAD

1 16-ounce can sauerkraut, drained and rinsed
1 4-ounce jar pimento, drained and chopped
1 cup onions, chopped
1 bell pepper, diced
½ cup vinegar
½ cup sugar

Combine all ingredients and mix well. Refrigerate overnight. Serves 6.
Mrs. Henry M. Burt (Lucy)
Mrs. Raymond Parks (Nada)

24 HOUR SALAD

"Great for a crowd."

1 large head iceberg lettuce
Salt and pepper to taste
¼ cup onion, chopped
¼ cup celery, chopped
1 6-ounce can water chestnuts, drained and sliced
1 16-ounce can English peas, well drained
2 cups Hellmann's mayonnaise
3 teaspoons sugar
½ pound Cheddar cheese, grated
¾ pound bacon, fried and crumbled
Tomato wedges or cherry tomatoes
3 to 4 hard-boiled eggs, sliced
Parsley

Shred lettuce in a large salad bowl and season with salt and pepper; sprinkle the next three ingredients over the lettuce. Place peas over the top. Spread mayonnaise like frosting and seal edges. Sprinkle on sugar and enough cheese to cover the top. Cover salad and refrigerate 24 hours. Before serving, top the salad with bacon, eggs, tomatoes, and parsley. Serves 10-15.
Mrs. Mario B. Papagni   Cullman, Alabama

Variation: Add a layer of 2 cups sliced carrots cooked until crisp and a layer of ⅔ cup sliced pimiento-stuffed olives for a different flavor.
Mrs. L. Daniel Bentley   Oneonta, Alabama

Variation: For another topping, mix 1 cup mayonnaise and 1 cup sour cream.
Mrs. Helen Orser   Opelika, Alabama

Variation: Add a layer of bell pepper rings and ¼ cup capers with 1 4-ounce can Parmesan cheese sprinkled over the mayonnaise topping instead of sugar to make a different version of this salad.
Mrs. James D. Luker (Judy)

CUCUMBERS IN SOUR CREAM

"Double this when cucumbers are plentiful."

½ pint sour cream
2 tablespoons cider vinegar
½ teaspoon salt
½ teaspoon ground dill (or dill seed)
2 tablespoons onion, chopped
Paprika to color
2 medium cucumbers

Combine first six ingredients in a quart container; mix well. Peel cucumbers and slice thin; add to sour cream mixture. Chill in refrigerator 3 or 4 hours before serving. Serves 4-6.
Mrs. William C. Hurst, Jr. (Sandra)

SPINACH-BACON SALAD BOWL FOR 18

18 (yes 18) cloves garlic, quartered
2¼ cups French dressing
9 eggs, hard-boiled
24 bacon slices
3 pounds (6 quarts) crisp young spinach, well-washed

About two hours ahead of serving time add garlic to French dressing; shell the hard-boiled eggs. Fry bacon and drain on paper towel. Refrigerate dressing, eggs, and bacon. At serving time chop eggs and crumble bacon; sprinkle both over spinach. Remove the garlic from the dressing and pour over the salad and toss. Serve at once. Serves 18.
Mrs. A. Stratton Lawrence (Elsie)

STUFFED TOMATO SALAD

6 medium tomatoes
4 ounces cream cheese
½ medium onion, chopped
½ medium bell pepper, chopped
Salt and pepper to taste
Tabasco to taste
Mayonnaise
Paprika

Peel tomatoes by dropping in boiling water a few seconds; then remove skin. (It is important to remove tomatoes quickly from the water.) Cream thoroughly the cream cheese. Add onion and bell pepper; mix thoroughly. Season with salt, pepper, and Tabasco to taste. Cut peeled tomatoes diagonally being sure not to cut too deeply. Fill tomatoes with cream cheese stuffing. Top each tomato with a small amount of mayonnaise and sprinkle with paprika. Serve on lettuce. Serves 6.
Mrs. Turner J. Jones (Katherine)

CAESAR SALAD

1 large bunch Romaine lettuce
½ cup olive oil
1 egg
½ teaspoon salt
1 teaspoon monosodium glutamate
½ teaspoon Tabasco
1 cup garlic bread croutons
Juice of ½ lemon
¼ cup Romano cheese, freshly grated
Pepper to taste

Tear off lettuce leaves. Wash well, drain and put in refrigerator to chill. Combine olive oil, egg, salt, monosodium glutamate and Tabasco in a small bowl; beat lightly. Add croutons to this mixture and stir briefly. Pour over torn lettuce and toss well. Add lemon juice, cheese and pepper to salad and toss again. Serve immediately. Serves 4.
Mrs. William W. Lawrence (Sally)

COLD CAULIFLOWER AND CHEESE SALAD

"Absolutely fantastic!"

6 heads cauliflower, cut into flowerets
4 cups mayonnaise
¾ cup sour cream
1 jar Dijon mustard
2 medium yellow onions, minced
Salt and pepper to taste
½ pound sharp Cheddar cheese, cut into small strips
Fresh parsley, chopped

Cook cauliflower in boiling salted water about 4 minutes. Drain. Mix mayonnaise, sour cream, and mustard until creamy. Add onion, salt and pepper; pour over cauliflower making sure it's well coated. Gently toss in cheese, reserving some for the top. Place in serving dish and insert pieces of cheese over top. Chill. Garnish with parsley. This recipe is easy to cut down. It keeps well and gets better as it seasons. Serves 20.
Mrs. L. T. Williams, Jr. (Charlotte)

SESAME LETTUCE SALAD

"A big hit with company."

2 tablespoons sesame seed, toasted
½ cup mayonnaise
½ cup French salad dressing
2 tablespoons Parmesan cheese, grated
1 tablespoon sugar
1 tablespoon vinegar
½ teaspoon salt
1 small head lettuce, torn up in bite size pieces
½ cup bell pepper, chopped
2 green onions, sliced
1 11-ounce can mandarin oranges, drained
½ medium cucumber, sliced

In skillet toast sesame seed until lightly browned; set aside. Combine mayonnaise, French dressing, cheese, sugar, vinegar and salt; add sesame seed. Combine lettuce, bell pepper and onions. Arrange lettuce mixture, orange sections and cucumber in salad bowl. Pour salad dressing on top; toss lightly before serving. Serves 4-6.
George R. Burton, Jr.

HOT GERMAN POTATO SALAD

"Warmer Kartoffelsalat"

4 medium potatoes
¼ pound bacon
¼ cup bacon fat
¼ cup onion, minced
2 tablespoons sugar
2 tablespoons flour
⅔ cup water
⅓ cup vinegar
1 egg, slightly beaten
¾ teaspoon salt

Cook potatoes in jackets in salted water until fork tender. Remove skin and slice potatoes while as hot as possible. Fry bacon until crisp. Remove, crumble into bits, and set aside. Drain off fat except ¼ cup. Return to heat, add onions, and sauté until golden brown. Stir sugar and flour into fat and onions; blend well. Reduce heat; stir in water and vinegar. Add egg and salt, stirring to blend thoroughly. Boil one minute. Add bacon and potatoes. Mix gently to coat with dressing. Remove from heat and serve hot. Serves 4.

Mrs. Larry Barksdale (Fran)

FRIED RICE SALAD

"A different potato for grilled steaks."

1 6¼-ounce package Chun King Stir-Fry Rice Mix
1½ cups celery, chopped
1 8½-ounce can water chestnuts, drained and sliced
⅓ cup Italian or French dressing

Prepare the rice according to package directions. Cool; then toss with the other ingredients. Chill at least 2 hours before serving. Serve chilled. Serves 4.

Mrs. Joe Woodard (Jerry)

SOUR CREAM POTATO SALAD

6 cups cooked potatoes, diced
¼ cup chopped green onions and tops
1 teaspoon celery seed
1½ teaspoons salt
½ teaspoon pepper
4 hard-boiled eggs
1 cup dairy sour cream
½ cup mayonnaise
¼ cup vinegar
1 teaspoon prepared mustard
¾ cup cucumber, diced
Parsley

Combine potatoes, onions, celery seed, salt, and pepper. Toss lightly. Separate whites of hard-boiled eggs from yolks; chop whites and add to potato mixture. Chill. Mash hard-cooked yolks; add sour cream, mayonnaise, vinegar and mustard. Mix well. Pour dressing over potatoes; toss lightly. Let stand 20 minutes. Just before serving, add cucumber. Trim with minced parsley. Serves 6.

Mrs. G. L. Kipps (Barbara)

ITALIAN POTATO SALAD

"A real man pleaser."

14 to 15 large red potatoes
½ cup parsley, chopped
½ cup green onion, chopped
3 large garlic pods, sliced thin or ¾ teaspoon garlic juice
½ teaspoon dry mustard
1 scant tablespoon sugar
1 tablespoon Worcestershire sauce
1 8-ounce bottle olive oil
½ cup tarragon vinegar

Boil potatoes; when fork tender, peel and cut into 1 inch chunk pieces. Sprinkle parsley and green onion over potatoes. Make dressing from remaining ingredients. Strain the dressing to remove pieces of garlic; then pour over potatoes. Stir well. Let stand 4 hours or more and stir every hour. Do NOT refrigerate. Serves 16.
Mrs. William B. McGehee, III (Evelyn)

CHINESE VEGETABLE SALAD

1 16-ounce can bean sprouts, drained
1 16-ounce can Chinese vegetables, drained
1 16-ounce can French green beans, drained
1 4-ounce can sliced mushrooms, drained
1 8½-ounce can water chestnuts, sliced and drained
2 stalks celery, sliced
1 large purple onion, sliced
1 2-ounce jar pimento, drained and chopped
1 bell pepper, sliced in rings

Drain and chop necessary vegetables and put in large bowl.

Dressing:

¾ cup sugar
1 cup white vinegar
½ teaspoon salt
¼ teaspoon pepper
½ cup oil
½ teaspoon celery seed

Boil vinegar and sugar until sugar is dissolved; add the other dressing ingredients. Pour mixture over vegetables and refrigerate at least 12 hours. Drain before serving. Serves 8-10.
Mrs. William W. Lawrence (Sally)

Similar recipes submitted by:
Ms. Jean Thornton
Mrs. Wallace Twiggs (Linda)

MEXICAN CHEF SALAD

"A complete meal for 4."

1 onion, chopped finely
4 tomatoes, peeled and chopped
1 head lettuce
1 avocado, cubed
2 teaspoons hot chili sauce
4 ounces cheese, grated or cubed
1 pound ground beef
1 16-ounce can kidney beans
1 large bag tortilla chips
French dressing

In a large bowl place chopped onion and tomatoes. Tear lettuce into pieces and add to same bowl. Add 1 cubed avocado, hot chili sauce and cheese. The recipe may be prepared in advance to this point. Brown ground beef and drain. Add (rinsed and drained) kidney beans; cook meat and beans 10 minutes. Cool and mix with salad mixture; add ½ bag of crushed tortilla chips. Serve with French dressing and tortilla chips. Serves 4.
Mrs. Frederick C. Hahn, Jr. (Martha)

RITZ CRACKER SLAW

"Try this flavorful slaw stuffed in a tomato."

1 medium cabbage, grated
1 medium onion, chopped finely
⅔ cup celery, chopped
⅔ cup bell pepper, chopped
2 packages Ritz crackers, crushed (2 out of 3 stack box)
2 tablespoons pickle relish
2 cups mayonnaise
4 tablespoons mustard
Salt and pepper to taste
1 cup sharp cheese, grated

Grate or chop cabbage; chop onion, celery and bell pepper. Crush crackers. Mix all ingredients together except cheese. Place grated cheese on top of slaw. Chill. Serves 12-15.
Mrs. Stephen F. Syer (Marion)

SLAW WITH HOT DRESSING

"A great accompaniment for any picnic or cookout."

1 medium cabbage
1 stalk celery
1 bell pepper
1 medium onion

Dressing:

1 egg
⅔ cup sugar
2 heaping tablespoons flour
1 teaspoon salt
½ teaspoon turmeric
½ cup vinegar
1 tablespoon margarine

Chop cabbage, celery, bell pepper and onion. Place celery, bell pepper, onion and ½ of the cabbage in a large bowl. In medium saucepan beat egg; add other ingredients for dressing except margarine and cook until thick. Add margarine and cook until it will leave sides of pan. Pour hot dressing over vegetables in bowl. Chill in refrigerator at least one hour; then add remaining chopped cabbage. Will last several days.
Mrs. O. Stanley Thornton (Cathy)

SWEET AND SOUR SLAW

1 large cabbage, shredded
3 stalks celery, chopped
1 bell pepper, chopped
1 4-ounce jar pimento, chopped
1 large red onion, shredded
½ cup red wine vinegar
½ cup white vinegar
¾ cup sugar
1½ teaspoons salt
¾ cup salad oil
Coarsely ground black pepper

Layer cabbage, celery, bell pepper, pimento, and onion in bowl. Boil vinegar, sugar, and salt for 2 minutes. Remove from heat; add salad oil and coarsely ground black pepper; return to heat and bring to a boil. Pour over vegetables while hot. Cover tightly. Refrigerate overnight. If refrigerated, this will keep indefinitely. Serves 10-12.
Mrs. Walter Burt (Brenda)
Similar recipes submitted by:
Mrs. James Barnett (Lynn)
Mrs. James F. Camp (Gayle)
Mrs. Hugo Molliston (Marion)
Mrs. Myron B. Waits (Miller)

SWEET AND SOUR VEGETABLE SALAD

1 16-ounce can cut green beans
1 16-ounce can yellow wax beans
1 15-ounce can red kidney beans
1 medium size onion, sweet red or white
2 cups fresh cauliflower, cut in bite size
1 bell pepper, cut in rings
8 to 10 radishes, sliced
1½ cups sugar
1⅓ cups vinegar
⅔ cup salad oil
2 teaspoons salt
2 teaspoons pepper

Rinse well and drain all three cans of beans through colander. Peel and cut onion in thin slices. Prepare other vegetables as directed above and mix in large bowl. Mix sugar, vinegar, oil, salt and pepper together to make marinade. Pour marinade over vegetables and chill overnight or for several hours. This can be kept in the refrigerator for several days. Serves 16-20.
Miss Martha Williams.

GREEN BEAN SALAD

1 16-ounce can French style beans, drained
1 17-ounce can English peas, drained
1 4-ounce jar pimento, chopped
1 bell pepper, chopped
1½ cups celery, chopped
2 or 3 small onions, chopped
¾ cup sugar
¾ cup vinegar
1 teaspoon salt
½ cup vegetable oil

Drain beans and peas. Add chopped pimento, bell pepper, celery, and onions. Heat sugar and vinegar until sugar is dissolved. Let cool. Add salt and vegetable oil. Pour over vegetables. Marinate for 24 hours. Drain before serving. This will keep for several days after it is marinated. Serves 8-10.
Mrs. C. L. Kelley (Hattie)
Similar recipes submitted by:
Mrs. T. C. Copeland (Barbara)
Mrs. Danny Harris (Joan)

CUCUMBER MOUSSE

"A cool, cool salad for a summertime lunch."

2 envelopes unflavored gelatin
1 cup cold water
¼ cup vinegar
⅔ cup mayonnaise
¾ teaspoon salt
⅛ teaspoon black pepper
2 cups cucumber, chopped
1 tablespoon onion, grated
1 cup heavy cream, whipped

Soften gelatin in 1 cup cold water; add vinegar. Stir over low heat until gelatin is dissolved. Cool. Gradually add mayonnaise, salt and pepper. Mix well and chill. When mayonnaise mixture is partially set (it sets quick), fold in cucumber, onion, and whipped cream. Pour into oiled mold. Chill. Serves 8.

Mrs. Charles Nelson (Mary)

JELLIED ARTICHOKES

2 cooked artichokes or 1 8½-ounce can artichokes
2 10½-ounce cans beef consommé
2 envelopes of unflavored gelatin
Juice of 2 lemons
Tabasco to taste
Salt and pepper to taste

Cut hearts into small pieces. If fresh artichokes are used, add the scrapings from leaves. Warm consommé; add gelatin which has been softened in cold water (see package directions). Season with lemon juice, Tabasco, salt, and pepper. Add artichokes. Pour into greased mold and refrigerate. Serve on lettuce with mayonnaise. Serves 8.

Mrs. William Larkin Coker, Jr. (Hattie Wallace)

BROCCOLI SALAD

"A different vegetable on a luncheon plate!"

2 10-ounce packages chopped frozen broccoli
1 envelope unflavored gelatin
1 10¾-ounce can beef consommé
Juice of 2 lemons
2 shakes Tabasco
Salt and red pepper to taste
2 hard-boiled eggs, sliced
¾ cup mayonnaise

Cook and drain broccoli. Soften gelatin in ¼ cup comsommé. Heat remainder of consommé and dissolve the softened gelatin in heated consommé. Cool. Add seasonings; fold in mayonnaise and broccoli. In the bottom of a greased loaf pan or mold, place half of the sliced hard-boiled eggs. Pour ½ of the broccoli mixture over eggs; add another layer of sliced eggs and cover with the remainder of broccoli. Place in refrigerator to congeal. Serves 10.

Mrs. Roy Evans (Johnnie)

VEGETABLE ASPIC

2 envelopes unflavored gelatin
1 cup cold water
2 cups boiling water
⅓ cup sugar
¼ cup mixed vinegar and lemon juice
¼ teaspoon salt
1 8½-ounce can artichoke hearts
1 16-ounce can French cut string beans, drained
½ cup celery, chopped
1 8-ounce can green peas, drained

Sprinkle gelatin on cold water to soften. Add sugar, mixed lemon juice and vinegar, salt and boiling water; stir until gelatin is dissolved. Cut artichokes in half. Pour small amount of gelatin mixture in bottom of greased mold. Place artichoke halves in center of mold. Put mold in refrigerator to set. Meanwhile, let remainder of aspic thicken. When aspic is syrupy, add string beans, celery and green peas. Pour this mixture on top of artichokes in mold. Refrigerate to set. Serve with mayonnaise to which horseradish and sour cream has been added. Serves 8-10.
Mrs. William Larkin Coker, III (Joan)

WATERGATE SALAD

1 9-ounce carton Cool Whip
1 7½-ounce can crushed pineapple with juices
1 cup miniature marshmallows
¾ cup nuts, chopped (optional)
1 3¾-ounce package Jello Pistachio Instant Pudding mix

Mix all ingredients together. Pour in ungreased shallow casserole. Chill until set. Serves 6-8.
Mrs. John Barksdale (Dot)
Mrs. Randall Stewart (Reba)

ASPARAGUS MOUSSE

1 10½-ounce can asparagus tips
1 envelope unflavored gelatin
½ teaspoon salt
Pinch of cayenne pepper
Juice of 1 lemon
1 pint of whipping cream, whipped
Almonds or pecans (optional)

Drain asparagus and reserve juice. Soften gelatin in ¼ cup asparagus juice and dissolve over heat. Mash asparagus. Add salt, cayenne pepper, and dissolved gelatin. Then add lemon juice. Chill. When mixture begins to thicken, fold in whipped cream. Add almonds or pecans. Put in small greased molds. Serve on lettuce with mayonnaise. Serves 6.
Mrs. H. Eugene Caldwell (Nell)

ASHEVILLE SALAD

"Very rich and delicious."

1 10¾-ounce can tomato soup, undiluted
1 soup can water
1 8-ounce package cream cheese
2 envelopes unflavored gelatin
½ cup cold water
1 cup mayonnaise
1½ cups celery, chopped
½ teaspoon onion, chopped
3 hard-boiled eggs, chopped
¼ cup bell pepper, chopped
6 (or more) stuffed olives, chopped
Salt and pepper to taste

In a saucepan, combine soup and can of water. Bring to a boil. Add cream cheese; stir until smooth and thoroughly blended. Soften gelatin in ½ cup cold water. Dissolve in hot soup mixture. Cool. Stir in remaining ingredients. Pour into a 1½-quart greased mold. Chill until firm. Serve unmolded on a bed of watercress or lettuce. Serves 8-10
Mrs. Allen C. Jacobs (Hope)

Variation: For a main dish salad, substitute one 6½ or 9-ounce can of drained tuna for the hard-boiled eggs and olives.
Mrs. R. E. Mullins (JoAnn)

CHICKEN MOUSSE

3 envelopes unflavored gelatin
½ cup cold water
1 10¾-ounce can mushroom soup
2½ cups chicken broth
2 teaspoons salt
¼ teaspoon pepper
¾ cup mayonnaise
5 cups cooked chicken, diced
1½ cups celery, finely diced
1½ tablespoons parsley, chopped
1 teaspoon Worcestershire sauce
2 tablespoons lemon juice
2 tablespoons onion, grated
½ pint whipping cream, whipped

Soften gelatin in cold water. Combine soup, broth, salt and pepper; cook until hot and blended. Dissolve gelatin in hot mixture. Cool. Blend in mayonnaise. Add chicken, celery, parsley, Worcestershire sauce, lemon juice and onions. Whip cream and fold into mixture. Pour into 12 small individual greased molds. Chill 4-5 hours or overnight. Garnish with French dressing and olives or cocktail onions and serve on lettuce leaf. Serves 12.
Mrs. Blake Harris (Mary Catherine)

TOMATO ASPIC

2 envelopes unflavored gelatin
½ cup tomato juice
3½ cups tomato juice, heated
½ teaspoon salt
1 bay leaf
Dash of Tabasco
1 teaspoon onion, grated (optional)
½ teaspoon Italian herbs
2 cups solid ingredients choice of: chopped celery rib and leaves, chopped bell pepper, sliced green or black olives, chopped artichoke hearts or chopped avocado

Soak gelatin in ½ cup tomato juice. Do not stir. Leave until gelatin is transparent and has absorbed moisture. Put 3½ cups tomato juice in a saucepan and add salt, bay leaf, Tabasco, onion and Italian herbs. Simmer; remove bay leaf. Remove mixture from heat and add gelatin mixture to hot juice. Let cool to room temperature. Add solid ingredients. Pour into oiled 2-quart casserole or eight individual molds. Chill until firm. Unmold or cut before serving. Serves 8-10.
Mrs. N. Gary Conover (Mufett)

CHICKEN CURRY FRUIT SALAD

"Easy and flavorful."

2 fresh pineapples, cut up or 1 20-ounce can pineapple chunks
2½ cups chicken or turkey, diced
¾ cup celery, diced
¾ cup mayonnaise
2 tablespoons chutney
½ teaspoon curry
½ cup coconut
⅓ cup salted peanuts
1 banana, sliced
1 11-ounce can mandarin oranges, drained

Drain pineapple very well. Mix pineapple, chicken and celery and chill. Mix mayonnaise, chutney and curry and chill at the same time. Just before serving combine chicken mixture and mayonnaise mixture and add coconut and peanuts. Top with sliced banana and oranges. Serves 4-6.
Mrs. Alton B. James Mobile, Alabama

DELICIOUS CHICKEN SALAD

1 20-ounce can white cherries, sliced with juice
2 tablespoons vinegar
Chicken broth
1 3-ounce package lemon gelatin
1 cup celery, chopped
2 to 3 cups cooked chicken, chopped finely

Drain juice from cherries and pour into saucepan; add vinegar and enough chicken broth to make 2 cups of liquid. Heat to boiling point and dissolve gelatin in boiling liquid. Cool. In a greased 2-quart casserole alternate layers of jello with celery, chicken and sliced cherries. Refrigerate to congeal. Serves 8.
Mrs. Joe L. Wallis (Dot)

SALMON LUNCHEON SALAD

1½ cups flaked canned salmon
½ cup celery, sliced
½ cup ripe olives, diced
2 tablespoons lemon juice
3 tablespoons mayonnaise
Shredded lettuce
1 hard-boiled egg
Cucumber
Tomatoes

Mix together lightly the salmon, celery, olives, lemon juice and mayonnaise. Arrange in mounds on shredded lettuce. Top each salad with a lengthwise quarter of egg and a topknot of mayonnaise. Garnish with sliced cucumber and tomatoes. Serves 4.
Mrs. Crawford Nelson (Linda)

HOT CHICKEN SALAD

"Add a congealed salad and broccoli for lunch."

2 cups cooked chicken, coarsely diced
2 cups celery, diced
½ cup slivered almonds, toasted
¾ teaspoon salt
¼ teaspoon pepper
2 teaspoons onion, grated
1 cup mayonniase
½ cup American cheese, grated
1 cup crushed cracker crumbs or potato chips

Mix all ingredients together except crumbs. Pour into a greased 1-quart casserole. Top with crumbs; bake at 400 degrees for 40 minutes. Serves 6.
Mrs. James N. Montgomery (Ann)
Mrs. Joe Woodard (Jerry)
Similar recipe submitted by Mrs. Tom Copeland (Barbara)

CRABMEAT SALAD

2 envelopes unflavored gelatin
¼ cup cold water
2 3-ounce packages cream cheese
1 can mushroom soup
1 cup mayonnaise
1 small onion, grated
1 tablespoon Worcestershire sauce
½ teaspoon salt
1 cup crabmeat
1 cup celery, chopped

Soften gelatin in cold water. Combine cream cheese, soup, mayonnaise, onion, Worcestershire and salt in double boiler; heat until blended. Remove from heat and add gelatin; stir until gelatin is dissolved. Add crabmeat and celery. Pour into oiled mold and chill. Garnish with a slice of cranberry sauce. Serves 10-12.
Mrs. George E. Tucker (Dot)

BING CHERRY SALAD

2 3-ounce packages cherry gelatin
2 cups hot water
2 6-ounce bottles Coca Cola
1 9-ounce can crushed pineapple
1 20-ounce can pitted black cherries
1 cup pecans, chopped

Dissolve gelatin in hot water; then add Coca Cola and partially congeal mixture. Add fruit and pecans. Pour into greased mold. Chill until set. Serve on lettuce leaf garnished with mayonnaise. Serves 8-10.
Mrs. William J. Munroe (Rachel)

FILLED MANDARIN SALAD

"A heavenly salad – almost a dessert."

¼ cup cold water
1 envelope unflavored gelatin
2 3-ounce packages orange gelatin
2 cups hot water
Juice from 1 15¼-ounce can pineapple chunks
Juice from 2 11-ounce cans of mandarin oranges, drained
1 11-ounce can mandarin oranges, drained
1 pint orange sherbet

Soften unflavored gelatin in cold water. Dissolve orange gelatin in hot water and add softened unflavored gelatin. Add juices, oranges, and sherbet to mixture; stir until sherbet is melted. Pour into greased ring mold; chill until firm.

Filling:

1 11-ounce can mandarin oranges, drained
1 15¼-ounce can pineapple chunks, drained
1 cup coconut
1 cup miniature marshmallows
¼ cup sour cream

Mix ingredients for filling together. Fill center of unmolded congealed salad. Serves 12.
Mrs. James Barnett (Lynn)
Similar recipes submitted by:
Mrs. Tom Copeland (Barbara)
Mrs. Charles Nelson (Mary)

JANIE RUTH'S FAVORITE

2 3-ounce packages strawberry gelatin
2 cups boiling water
2 cups cold water
1 8-ounce package cream cheese, softened
1 cup pecans, chopped
1 16-ounce can crushed pineapple, drained
½ cup maraschino cherries, chopped
1 6¼-ounce bag miniature marshmallows

Dissolve gelatin according to package directions, using 9 x 11-inch pyrex dish or large mold. Chill until gelatin begins to thicken. Combine cream cheese, pineapple, cherries, and pecans in a large bowl; then add to gelatin. Mix until well blended; then top with marshmallows. Chill until firm. Serves 15-18.
Mrs. Hugo Molliston (Marion)

BLUEBERRY SALAD

1 16-ounce can blueberries with juice
1 8½-ounce can crushed pineapple with juice
1 3-ounce package black cherry gelatin
1 3-ounce package raspberry gelatin
2 cups boiling water

Drain blueberries and pineapple; reserve juice. Dissolve gelatin in boiling water. Add 1 cup pineapple and blueberry juice. Stir in drained fruit and pour into 2-quart dish (13½ x 8¾ x 1¾-inch). Refrigerate to congeal.

Topping:

1 8-ounce package cream cheese
½ cup sugar
1 pint sour cream
½ teaspoon vanilla
½ cup pecans, chopped

Soften cream cheese and fold in sugar, sour cream, vanilla, and pecans. Spread over congealed salad. Serves 12.
Mrs. Jack Clark (Becky)
Similar recipe submitted by:
Mrs. George Hartsfield (Linda)
Mrs. M. C. Britton Aleander City, Alabama

MILLION DOLLAR SALAD

"The name says it all."

1 6¼-ounce package miniature marshmallows
1 20-ounce can crushed pineapple, drained
2 tablespoons sugar
1 8-ounce package cream cheese
1 tablespoon mayonnaise
12 or more maraschino cherries, chopped
1 cup pecans, chopped, (optional)
1 cup heavy cream, whipped

Combine marshmallows and pineapple. Cream sugar, cream cheese and mayonnaise until well blended. Add pineapple mixture, cherries and pecans; fold in whipped cream. Place in 13 x 9 x 2-inch pan. Chill well. Serves 24.

Mrs. Larry Barksdale (Fran)

FROZEN GRAPEFRUIT SALAD

1 8-ounce package cream cheese
1 cup sour cream
¼ teaspoon salt
½ cup sugar
1 grapefruit, sectioned
1 avocado, diced
1 cup seedless white grapes, halved
½ cup pecans, chopped

Soften cream cheese and blend in sour cream. Add salt and sugar; stir until well blended. Add grapefruit sections, avocado, grapes, and pecans. Pour into 9 x 5-inch loaf pan and freeze until firm. Slice and serve on salad greens with French dressing. Serves 6-8.

Mrs. Jimmy Hall (Martha)

FROZEN CRANBERRY SALAD

1 16-ounce can jellied cranberry sauce
Juice of 1 lemon
½ pint whipping cream, whipped
¼ cup mayonnaise
¼ cup confectioners sugar
½ cup walnuts, chopped (optional)

Mash the cranberry sauce in the bottom of a greased ice tray and mold and sprinkle with the lemon juice. Whip cream; then add the mayonnaise and sugar. Pour over the cranberry mixture and freeze. When the salad is hard, cover it with foil until ready to cut in squares. Serves 6.

Mrs. James C. Peeples (Mary Frances)

APRICOT CHEESE SALAD

"Delight your bridge club with this."

1 16-ounce can apricots, drained and chopped finely
1 16-ounce can crushed pineapple, drained
2 3-ounce packages orange gelatin
2 cups hot water
1 cup apricot juice
1 cup miniature marshmallows

Drain apricots and pineapple, chill in separate bowl. Dissolve gelatin in hot water; add 1 cup of apricot juice. Cool; then fold in apricots, pineapple and marshmallows. Chill until firm.

Topping:

½ cup sugar
3 tablespoons flour
1 egg, slightly beaten
2 tablespoons butter
1 cup pineapple juice
1 cup whipping cream, whipped
¾ cup Cheddar cheese, grated

Mix thoroughly the sugar, flour, egg, butter, and pineapple juice. Cook over low heat until thick. Cool. Fold in whipped cream and spread over salad. Sprinkle with grated cheese. Cut in squares. Serves 15-18.
Mrs. Frank Harwell (Edith)

APRICOT SALAD

"A favorite with the ladies."

⅔ cup water
⅔ cup sugar
2 3-ounce packages apricot gelatin
1 8-ounce carton sour cream
1 8-ounce can crushed pineapple with juices
2 small jars apricot baby food or 1 junior size jar apricot baby food
1 4½-ounce carton Cool Whip
½ cup chopped nuts (optional)

Mix water and sugar with gelatin; bring to a boil until gelatin dissolves. Cool. Add sour cream, apricot baby food with crushed pineapple and juices. Fold in Cool Whip. Pour mixture into a 7 x 13-inch pan and refrigerate or freeze. It can be used as a congealed salad or frozen dessert.
Mrs. Tom Copeland (Barbara)
Mrs. Winston Legge (Sara)
Mrs. James White (Evelyn)
Similar recipes submitted by:
Mrs. Hugo Molliston (Marion)
Mrs. James N. Montgomery (Ann)

APPLE SALAD

2 3-ounce packages lemon gelatin
1 cup boiling water
2 cups cold water
2 cups apples, finely chopped
1 8-ounce can crushed pineapple with juices
2 cups miniature marshmallows
1 cup nuts, chopped

Dissolve gelatin in boiling water; add cold water. When gelatin is partially congealed, add remaining ingredients. Chill until firm.

Topping:

2 eggs, beaten
½ cup sugar
2 tablespoons lemon juice
1 envelope Dream Whip

Cook eggs, sugar, and lemon juice over low heat until thick. Cool. Prepare Dream Whip according to package directions; then fold it into cooked mixture. Spoon topping on salad and chill several hours before serving.
Mrs. Pope Wilder (Frances)

CONGEALED CRANBERRY SALAD

"A must for the Holidays."

1 16-ounce can whole cranberry sauce
1 cup boiling water
1 3-ounce package strawberry gelatin
2 tablespoons lemon juice
¼ teaspoon salt
½ cup mayonnaise
1 apple, diced
¼ cup walnuts or pecans, chopped

Heat cranberry sauce; strain. Mix cranberry juice, boiling water and gelatin; stirring until completely dissolved. Add lemon juice and salt. Chill mixture until slightly thickened. Add mayonnaise; beat with rotary beater until fluffy. Fold in cranberries, apple and nuts. Pour into greased mold and chill until firm. Serves 6.
Mrs. Carl R. Reaves (Joyce)
Similar recipe submitted by Mrs. R. E. Mullins (Jo Ann)

LUAU SALAD

"No leftovers when you serve this."

1 to 2 pints fresh strawberries
1 fresh pineapple (no substitute)
2 to 3 bananas, sliced
Lemon juice

Clean, halve, and sweeten strawberries. Peel and core pineapple; cut it into chunks, being sure to save juice. Combine strawberries and pineapple with juices in glass bowl. Refrigerate several hours. Just before serving add sliced bananas. Sprinkle with lemon juice and mix gently. Serves 6-8.

Mrs. W. H. Camp, Jr. (Betty Lou)

FRUIT SALAD

3 bananas, sliced
2 apples, cut in wedges
Melon balls (use ½ honeydew, ½ cantaloupe or ¼ watermelon)
1 11-ounce can mandarin oranges, drained
1 15½-ounce can pineapple chunks, drained
1 pint fresh strawberries
½ pound seedless white grapes

Place all the fruit in a large glass bowl.

Dressing:

2 cups Grenadine syrup
1 8-ounce carton sour cream
½ cup sugar

Mix all dressing ingredients with an electric mixer. Pour over fruit and chill. Serves 12-15.

Mrs. James W. Washam (Charlotte)

FRUIT SALAD OR DESSERT

1 4½-ounce carton Cool Whip
1 3¾-ounce package strawberry gelatin (any flavor of gelatin will do)
1 16-ounce carton cottage cheese
1 16-ounce can fruit cocktail, drained
1 7½-ounce can crushed pineapple, drained

Blend Cool Whip and dry gelatin together and add the carton of cottage cheese; mix well. Blend in drained fruit cocktail and pineapple. Chill.

Mrs. Curtis Lackey (Barbara)
Mrs. Stuart McConnell (Pat)

salad dressings

BLUE CHEESE DRESSING

"A treat for Blue Cheese lovers."

1 4-ounce package blue cheese
Juice of 2 lemons
1 pint mayonnaise
1 pint buttermilk
1 cup sour cream
1 tablespoon garlic powder
1 tablespoon onion powder

Soften blue cheese in lemon juice. Add remaining ingredients and mix well. Makes 1 quart.
Mrs. Tom Copeland (Barbara)

CELERY SEED DRESSING

"A different French dressing for fruit."

⅓ cup sugar
1 teaspoon salt
1 teaspoon paprika
1 teaspoon dry mustard
1 teaspoon celery seed
1 tablespoon onion, grated
2 tablespoons vinegar
1 cup salad oil

Combine all ingredients except salad oil in a bowl and mix well. Then slowly beat in 1 cup salad oil, drop by drop, until it begins to thicken. Chill overnight or several hours.
Mrs. James L. Hardwick (Dot)
Mrs. Graham Wright (Martee)

POPPYSEED DRESSING

"Delicious with fresh fruit."

1 teaspoon salt
½ cup sugar
1 teaspoon dry mustard
1 teaspoon paprika
¼ cup lemon juice
1 tablespoon poppyseeds
1 cup salad oil

In a medium size bowl mix all ingredients but the salad oil. Then with an electric mixer, beat the mixture slowly adding 1 cup of salad oil. Beat until it is the consistency of honey. This dressing keeps well in the refrigerator for several weeks.
Mrs. J. Wallis Elliott (Dede)

SPICY MUSTARD

"Delicious on sandwiches and in potato salad."

5 tablespoons dry mustard
½ cup sugar
1 tablespoon all-purpose flour
½ teaspoon salt
Dash of red pepper
2 eggs, beaten
½ cup vinegar
1 tablespoon butter

Combine mustard, sugar, flour, salt and red pepper in the top of a double boiler. Add eggs and vinegar, blending thoroughly. Place over boiling water; cook stirring constantly until thickened. Add butter; stir until melted. Cool mixture; then store in a jar in the refrigerator. Makes 1⅓ cups.
Mrs. George Hartsfield (Linda)

COOKED DRESSING

"Excellent for slaw or stuffed eggs."

2 eggs
2 tablespoons sugar
2 tablespoons butter
6 tablespoons vinegar
1 teaspoon salt
Pepper to taste
Celery seed to taste

Beat eggs until very light. Add sugar, vinegar, and butter and pour into saucepan. Cook slowly, stirring constantly until thick. Remove from stove and season with salt, pepper, and celery seed. Makes ½ cup.
Mrs. Raymond Hammett (Louise)

SATAN'S DRESSING

"Only 3½ calories per tablespoon."

1 cup tomato juice
¼ cup bell pepper, chopped
2 teaspoons Worcestershire sauce
1 teaspoon salt
1 teaspoon dry mustard
1 clove garlic, minced
½ teaspoon sugar
¼ cup vinegar

Combine all ingredients in a blender and blend on high speed until the bell pepper is pureed. Refrigerate. (Makes about 1½ cups.) Keeps well for about ten days.
Mrs. Carson Whitson (Sara)

BOBBY TOM'S SALAD DRESSING

2 small garlic cloves
3½ heaping tablespoons Hellmann's mayonnaise
4 ounces blue cheese, crumbled
¼ teaspoon celery salt
¼ teaspoon onion salt
½ teaspoon salt
½ teaspoon pepper
½ cup oil
2 heads lettuce

Rub a wooden salad bowl with garlic cloves cut in half. Remove all pieces of garlic and put all ingredients except oil in the bowl. Mix until smooth. In a separate bowl, toss greens with oil. Add greens to salad bowl and toss with dressing. Coating greens with oil keeps the lettuce from wilting. Salad should be mixed shortly before serving; however, the dressing can be stored in the refrigerator for several weeks.
Mrs. Robert Jenkins *Birmingham, Alabama*

pickles and relishes

WATERMELON PICKLES

"Adds a nice Southern touch to a meal."

4 tablespoons salt
1 gallon water
Rind of one medium-size watermelon, cut into bite-size pieces
1 tablespoon alum
1 gallon boiling water
4 quarts water
4 cups sugar
1 quart vinegar
6 pounds sugar
6 cinnamon sticks
1 tablespoon nutmeg
2 tablespoons cloves, tied
1 large bottle marschino cherries

Add 4 tablespoons of salt to 1 gallon of water. Pour over rind pieces and soak 3 hours. Pour off liquid. Add 1 tablespoon of alum to 1 gallon of boiling water. Pour over rind pieces and soak 3 hours. Pour off liquid. Make a syrup of 4 quarts water and 4 cups sugar. Pour over rinds and simmer slowly 6 hours. Drain and discard syrup. Make a syrup of 1 quart vinegar, 6 pounds sugar, 6 cinnamon sticks, 1 tablespoon nutmeg, 2 tablespoons cloves in a gauze bag and maraschino cherries. Bring this to a boil. Drop in the rind and let boil 5 minutes. Remove from fire; let stand 24 hours in a crock pottery container to become "plump". Then bring to a boil again and if the syrup is not thick enough let the fruit stand on a platter and boil the syrup down to desired thickness. Then pour syrup over fruit. Pack into sterile jars and seal.
Mrs. W. Clifford Hearn (Nell)

CRANBERRY FRUIT RELISH

"Double this recipe to share with friends for the Holidays!"

1 pound cranberries
2 large apples
2 oranges and the peeling of one
1 cup golden raisins
3 cups sugar
Nuts, chopped

Put all fruit through the food grinder and add sugar and nuts.
Mrs. William C. Hurst, Jr. (Sandra)

GARLIC CANDIED SWEET PICKLES

1 gallon sour (not dill) pickles
1 clove garlic, sliced
5 or 6 cinnamon sticks
5 pounds sugar
½ box mustard seed
3 tablespoons peppercorns

Drain well and slice pickles. Make layers of pickles and remaining ingredients in the gallon jar starting with the pickles. Place layer of pickles sprinkling with mustard seed, peppercorns, garlic slices and cinnamon sticks; then cover with a layer of sugar. Repeat this process until the jar is full. Refrigerate and keep adding sugar until the entire five pounds is used. Turn the jar occasionally to resettle sugar. All the sugar will dissolve and the pickles will be crisp and sweet. The entire process takes a day or two to complete.
Mrs. Joe Woodard (Jerry)

CHOW CHOW RELISH

6 or 8 bell peppers
5 or 6 onions
2 hot peppers
1 gallon tomatoes, peeled
1 pint vinegar
2 cups sugar
Pickling spices (size of walnut) wrapped in cheese cloth and tied

Chop vegetables; mix with vinegar and sugar. Simmer together 4 hours with pickling spices. Seal in sterilized jars. Makes 5 pints.
Mrs. Ray Edmiston (Kara)

RIPE TOMATO RELISH

36 large ripe tomatoes
12 large white onions
3 large bell peppers
1 quart white vinegar
2 teaspoons ground allspice
2 teaspoons celery seed
3 teaspoons salt
8 cups sugar

Peel and chop tomatoes, onions and peppers in chunks and place in a two gallon enamel boiler. Add vinegar, allspice, celery seed and salt. Boil this combination slowly, stirring often, until it cooks down and thickens, (about four hours). Add sugar continuing to stir and watch carefully making sure the mixture does not stick and scorch. Continue cooking and stirring for another hour. Pour into hot sterilized jars and seal. This is delicious on meats and vegetables. Makes 24 half pints.
Mrs. Sara W. Hammett (Sally)

BARBARA PICKLES

4 quarts cucumber slices, unpared
7 tablespoons plain salt, (not iodized)
1½ quarts apple cider vinegar
1 tablespoon celery seed
2 tablespoons mustard seeds
1½ teaspoons curry powder
4 cups sugar

Slice cucumbers fairly thin. Sprinkle slices with salt. Cover with cold water and let stand overnight. Drain and wash slices several times in clear water. Bring vinegar, seasonings and sugar to a boil. Add slices and heat 4 minutes. Stir constantly, being careful not to let boil. Pack at once into sterilized jars and seal.
Mrs. Julian L. Newman (Becky)

SQUASH PICKLES

8 cups small yellow squash, sliced
2 cups onion, thinly sliced
4 bell peppers, thinly sliced (2 green and 2 red for color, if possible)
Salt to taste
2 cups vinegar
3 cups sugar
2 teaspoons mustard seed
2 teaspoons celery seed

Mix squash, onion and bell peppers with salt to taste and let stand one hour. Drain well. Bring remainder of ingredients to a boil. Add squash, onion and pepper and bring back to a boil. Pack in hot sterile jars. Makes about 3 pints.
Mrs. Toby Deese (Ruth Helen)
Mrs. William C. Hurst, Jr. (Sandra)
Mrs. Jack Wright (Joyce)

DILL PICKLES

20-25 pickling-size cucumbers
1 quart white vinegar
2 quarts cold water
½ cup plain salt

PER QUART:

Dill
1 clove garlic
1 pod red pepper
Pinch of turmeric
Pinch of alum

Place washed cucumbers in a quart jar; add dill, garlic and red pepper to each jar. Then add turmeric and alum. Mix water, vinegar and salt in a saucepan and bring to a boil. Pour over cucumbers and fill to ½ inch of top of jar. Sterilize lids and jar tops and seal jars tightly. Store in a dark place for at least six weeks before serving.
Mrs. James C. Peeples (Mary Frances)
Similar recipe submitted by Mrs. James R. Crowell (Bonnie)

Manning Hall
Alabama School for Deaf and Blind
by Sara Hammett

Sweets

cakes

KEUCHEN

"For a German treat, try this with your coffee."

4 cups all-purpose flour, sifted
½ pound margarine
1 teaspoon salt
⅓ package dry yeast
⅓ cup lukewarm water
1 cup cream
4 egg yolks, beaten
4 tablespoons sugar
4 egg whites, stiffly beaten
1 cup sugar
½ teaspoon vanilla
½ teaspoon almond flavoring
Pecans, chopped

Mix first three ingredients together thoroughly. In small bowl, combine yeast and water; stir until dissolved. In another bowl, combine cream, egg yolks, and sugar; mix well. Combine all three mixtures. Divide dough into four parts. Place each piece on wax paper and roll into rectangles. Beat egg whites until stiff; add sugar and flavorings while beating. Spread egg white mixture over half each rectangle; sprinkle with pecans; fold remaining dough over; seal edges. Place on wax paper covered baking sheet. Bake in 350 degree oven for 25 minutes. Top with icing and almonds.

ICING:

1 cup confectioners' sugar
1 teaspoon almond flavoring
Water
Almonds, slivered

Mix sugar with flavoring and enough water to make spreadable. Spread on keuchen and sprinkle with almonds.
Mrs. Robert Mullins (JoAnn)

BANANA SPLIT CAKE

"A pretty but very rich dessert – good for club meetings."

2 cups graham crackers, crushed
6 tablespoons margarine, melted
2 cups confectioners' sugar
½ cup margarine, softened
2 eggs
1 teaspoon vanilla
3 large bananas, sliced
1 20-ounce can pineapple, crushed, drained
1 13½-ounce container Cool Whip
½ cup nuts, chopped
6 maraschino cherries, halved

Combine first two ingredients; press into 9 x 13 x 2-inch pan. Bake in 350 degree oven for 7 minutes. Cool. In mixing bowl, cream sugar and margarine. Add eggs and vanilla and beat on high speed until fluffy. Spread over crust; cover with bananas, pineapple, and Cool Whip. Top with nuts and cherries. Store in refrigerator. Serves 15-18.

Mrs. Esther DeAngelis Harrisburg, Pennsylvania
Mrs. Stanley Thornton (Cathy)

LINDY'S CHEESECAKE

1 cup flour, sifted
¼ cup sugar
1 teaspoon lemon peel, grated
½ cup margarine
1 egg yolk, slightly beaten
¼ teaspoon vanilla
5 8-ounce packages cream cheese
1¾ cups sugar
3 tablespoons flour
¾ teaspoon lemon peel, grated
¼ teaspoon salt
¼ teaspoon vanilla
5 eggs
2 egg yolks
¼ cup heavy cream

Combine flour, sugar, and lemon peel. Cut in margarine until mixture is crumbly. Add egg yolk and vanilla; blend well. Pat one third dough out on bottom 9-inch spring form pan with sides removed. Bake in 400 degree oven for 8 minutes. Cool. Grease sides of pan and attach bottom. Pat remaining dough evenly on sides. Stir cheese to soften; beat until fluffy. Combine sugar, flour, lemon peel, salt, and vanilla. Add to cheese and mix. Add eggs and yolks, one at a time, beating after each addition. Gently stir in cream. Pour into pan. Bake at 450 degrees for 12 minutes or until top edge is golden. Reduce heat to 300 degrees and bake 55 minutes or until knife comes out clean. Cool in pan at least 3 hours. Remove sides. Store in refrigerator. May be served plain or with fruit glaze.

Mrs. John Q. Adams (Sara)

BROWN SUGAR POUND CAKE

"This is also good with caramel icing."

3 sticks margarine
1 box plus 1 cup dark brown sugar
5 eggs
3½ cups flour
½ teaspoon baking powder
½ teaspoon salt
1 cup milk
1 teaspoon vanilla
½ teaspoon maple flavoring
½ cup pecans, chopped

Cream margarine until fluffy. Add sugar and cream well. Add eggs, one at a time, beating after each addition. Sift flour, baking powder, and salt. Add dry ingredients alternately with milk. Add flavorings and nuts. Pour into well greased and floured tube pan. Bake in 325 degree oven for 1½ hours.
Mrs. Walter Burt (Brenda)

"COMPANY'S COMING" COCONUT CAKE

"Tastes like an old timey fresh coconut cake."

2 6-ounce packages frozen coconut
1 8-ounce carton sour cream
1½ cups sugar
1 box Duncan Hines yellow cake mix
1 4-ounce box instant vanilla pudding
½ cup cooking oil
1 cup water
1 teaspoon vanilla
2 eggs
2 egg yolks

Combine first three ingredients and set aside. In mixing bowl, combine remaining ingredients and beat until smooth. Pour into 2 greased 9-inch cake pans. Bake in 350 degree oven for 30 minutes. Cool 10 minutes on rack. Split layers to make four. Spread coconut mixture between layers while warm. Ice cake.

ICING:

2 egg whites
¾ cup sugar
⅓ cup white Karo syrup
1 tablespoon water
¼ teaspoon cream tartar
¼ teaspoon salt
¼ teaspoon vanilla
1 3½-ounce can coconut

In double boiler, combine first six ingredients and cook for 5 minutes, beating constantly at high speed. Remove from heat; add vanilla. Spread over cake and sprinkle with coconut.
Mrs. Patrick Duke (Carolyn)

CHOCOLATE CHERRY GATEAU

3 4-ounce bars German's Sweet chocolate
1 pound butter
3 tablespoons light Karo syrup
4 egg yolks
2 tablespoons rum (optional)
1 pound Lorna Doones or graham crackers, crushed
½ cup nuts, chopped
1 4-ounce carton candied cherries
½ cup whipping cream, whipped

In double boiler, melt chocolate. In saucepan, melt butter over low heat; add syrup. Cool slightly. In large mixing bowl, beat egg yolks lightly and slowly add butter mixture while stirring. Add chocolate and rum and beat well. Fold in cookie or cracker crumbs. Add nuts and cherries, reserving few to decorate slices. Grease spring form pan, with removable bottom, and spoon in cake mixture. Chill in refrigerator overnight. Slice and serve topped with whipped cream. Sprinkle with nuts and cherries.
Mrs. Carl Stockton (Jill)

ORANGE DATE CAKE

"Be sure to use butter – it makes a difference!"

1 cup butter
2 cups sugar
4 eggs
1 teaspoon soda
⅓ cup buttermilk
4 cups flour
1 pound dates, chopped
1 cup pecans, chopped
2 tablespoons orange rind, grated

Cream butter and sugar. Beat in eggs, one at a time. Dissolve soda in buttermilk. Dredge dates and pecans in small amount of flour. Add flour and buttermilk alternately to creamed mixture. Add remaining ingredients; blend well. Pour into greased tube pan. Bake in 325 degree oven for 1½ hours. Make tiny holes in top of cake and cover with sauce. Cool in pan. When cooled, loosen edges with knife before turning out on to cake plate. Cake is very tender. Garnish with orange sections.

SAUCE:

2 cups sugar
1 cup orange juice
2 tablespoons orange rind, grated

Mix all ingredients until dissolved. Pour over cake.
Mrs. Carl Monroe (Sula)

ITALIAN CREAM CAKE

1 stick margarine
½ cup shortening
2 cups sugar
5 egg yolks
2 cups flour
1 teaspoon soda
1 cup buttermilk
1 teaspoon vanilla
1 cup coconut, shredded
1 cup nuts, chopped
5 egg whites, stiffly beaten

Cream margarine and shortening; add sugar and beat until smooth. Add egg yolks and beat well. Combine flour and soda; add to creamed mixture alternately with buttermilk. Stir in vanilla. Add coconut and nuts; mix well. Fold in egg whites. Pour into greased and floured 9 x 13 x 2-inch pan or 3 8-inch pans. Bake in 350 degree oven 9 x 13 x 2-inch pan 45-50 minutes or 25-30 minutes for 8-inch pans. Cool. Top with frosting.

FROSTING:

1 8-ounce package cream cheese, softened
½ stick margarine
1 teaspoon vanilla
1 box confectioners' sugar
½ cup nuts, chopped

Beat cream cheese and margarine until smooth. Add remaining ingredients and mix well. Spread over cooled cake.
Mrs. Wayne Washam (Charlotte)

MARBLE CHOCOLATE POUND CAKE

1 cup Crisco
3 cups sugar
6 eggs
3 cups flour, sifted
½ teaspoon salt
¼ teaspoon soda
1 cup buttermilk
1 teaspoon vanilla
1 5-ounce can chocolate syrup

Cream Crisco, sugar, and eggs. Sift together flour, salt, and soda. Add buttermilk and dry ingredients alternately beginning and ending with buttermilk. Add vanilla. Pour one half of batter into greased tube pan. Add syrup to remaining batter; drop by spoonsful on top of batter in pan. Swirl. Bake in 350 degree oven for 1 hour.
Mrs. Jack Landham (Joan)

CARROT CAKE

2 cups all-purpose flour
2 cups sugar
2 teaspoons soda
2 teaspoons cinnamon
½ teaspoon salt
1½ cup Wesson oil
4 eggs
3 cups carrots, grated

Sift together dry ingredients. Add oil and eggs and beat well. Add carrots. Pour into 3 8-inch or 2 9-inch greased and floured cake pans. Bake in 350 degree oven for 25 minutes. Cool before icing.

ICING:

1 8-ounce package cream cheese
1 stick margarine
2 teaspoons vanilla
1 cup pecans, chopped
1½ cups confectioners' sugar

Variation: ½ cup pecans, chopped and ½ cup raisins softened in hot water may be added to cake mixture.
Mrs. Graham Wright (Martee)

FRESH APPLE CAKE

"A good holiday cake."

2 cups sugar
1¼ cups Wesson oil
3 eggs
3 cups all-purpose flour
1 teaspoon salt
1 teaspoon soda
3 teaspoon vanilla or lemon flavoring
3 cups apples, chopped
1 cup pecans or walnuts, chopped

In mixing bowl, beat sugar, oil, and eggs for 3 minutes on medium speed. Mix dry ingredients and slowly add to egg mixture. Fold in flavoring, apples, and nuts. Pour into greased tube pan or 9 x 13 x 2-inch pan. Bake in 350 degree oven for 50 minutes or until done. Pour on glaze while hot. Cool in pan.

GLAZE:

1 cup dark brown sugar
¼ cup milk
1 stick margarine

In saucepan, combine all ingredients and bring to boil. Boil for 3 minutes. Pour over cake.
Mrs. Larry Womack *Birmingham, Alabama*

CHOCOLATE MOCHA TORTE

"For the most fancy birthday cake!"

¾ cup flour, sifted
½ teaspoon baking powder
½ teaspoon salt
2 ½ ounces unsweetened chocolate, melted
6 eggs
¾ cup sugar
¼ cup cold water
¼ teaspoon soda
2 tablespoons sugar
Confectioners' sugar

Sift flour, baking powder, and salt together. Melt chocolate. Let eggs become room temperature; beat until thick; gradually add sugar while beating. Add flour mixture, all at once, and blend with wire whisk. Combine chocolate, water, soda, and sugar; stir until smooth. Quickly fold into batter. Grease and line with greased wax paper 15 x 10x 1-inch jelly roll pan. Pour batter into pan and bake in 350 degree oven for 20 minutes. Turn cake onto towel sprinkled with confectioners' sugar. Remove paper. Cool and cut into four equal parts. Split each part to make eight thin layers. Ice layers. Must be made several hours in advance of serving.

ICING:

2 tablespoons instant coffee
2 tablespoons hot milk
⅔ cup butter
1 box confectioners' sugar
2 egg whites, unbeaten
1 teaspoon vanilla

Dissolve coffee in milk. Cream butter and add 1 cup sugar. Combine mixtures and blend well. Add remaining sugar, egg whites, and vanilla. Blend well. Spread between layers and sides of cake.

GLAZE:

1 square unsweetened chocolate
1 tablespoon butter
1½ tablespoons hot milk
½ cup confectioners' sugar, sifted
Dash salt

Melt chocolate and butter over low heat. Combine milk, sugar, and salt. Add chocolate mixture gradually, mixing well. Spread over torte and dribble down sides. Chill several hours before serving. Serves 12.

Mrs. James Heacock, Jr. (Harriet)

STRAWBERRY CREAM CAKE

1 box Duncan Hines Deluxe II yellow cake mix
1 4-ounce box instant vanilla pudding
½ cup oil
1 cup water
2 eggs
2 egg yolks
1 teaspoon vanilla

In mixing bowl, combine all ingredients and beat until smooth. Pour in to 2 greased 9 inch pans. Bake at 350 degrees for 25 - 30 minutes. Cool. Split layers to make four. Spread layers with filling.

FILLING:

3 pints fresh strawberries
3 tablespoons sugar
3 cups heavy cream
¾ to 1 cup powdered sugar
¾ teaspoon vanilla

Wash and slice strawberries; sprinkle with sugar and set aside. In small bowl, beat cream, powdered sugar, and vanilla. Place brown side of one layer on plate; cover with cream filling and top with strawberries. Repeat layers. Use remaining cream filling to cover sides. Serves 12-15.
Mrs. James Barnett (Lynn)

FESTIVE CAKE

3 cups all-purpose flour
2 cups sugar
1 teaspoon baking soda
1 teaspoon salt
1 teaspoon cinnamon
1 cup nuts, chopped
3 eggs
1½ cups vegetable oil
1 teaspoon almond extract
2 cups bananas, chopped
1 8-ounce can crushed pineapple

Sift together dry ingredients; stir in nuts. Beat eggs slightly; combine with remaining ingredients. Add to dry ingredients; mix thoroughly, but do not beat. Spoon into well greased 10 inch tube pan. Bake in 325 degree oven for 1 hour 20 minutes. Remove from oven; let stand 10-15 minutes; invert on to wire cake rack. Cool before frosting.

FROSTING:

1 8-ounce package cream cheese, softened
½ cup butter
1 box confectioners' sugar
1 tablespoon instant chocolate

Combine all ingredients and mix well. Spread over cake. Store in refrigerator until ready to serve.
Mrs. James Luker (Judy)

CREAM CHEESE POUND CAKE

3 sticks margarine
3 cups sugar
1 8-ounce package cream cheese
6 egg yolks
3 cups flour
¼ teaspoon soda
1 teaspoon flavoring
6 egg whites, beaten

Cream margarine, sugar, and cream cheese. Add egg yolks, one at a time, beating after each addition. Add flour, soda, and flavoring. Fold in beaten egg whites. Pour into greased tube pan. Bake in 300 degree oven for 1½ hours or until done.
Mrs. Robert Mullins (JoAnn)

CHOCOLATE SHEET CAKE

2 cups sugar
2 cups flour
¼ teaspoon salt
1 stick margarine
½ cup shortening
4 tablespoons cocoa
1 cup water
1 teaspoon soda
½ cup buttermilk
2 eggs, slightly beaten
1 teaspoon cinnamon
1 teaspoon vanilla

Sift sugar, flour, and salt into large bowl. In saucepan, combine margarine, shortening, cocoa, and water and bring to rapid boil. Pour over flour mixture and add remaining ingredients. Mix well by hand. Pour into greased 16 x 11-inch pan. Bake in 400 degree oven for 20 minutes. Top with icing.

ICING:

1 stick margarine
4 tablespoons cocoa
6 tablespoons milk
1 box confectioners' sugar
1 teaspoon vanilla
1 cup nuts, chopped

In saucepan, combine margarine, cocoa, and milk and bring to rapid boil. Remove from heat; add sugar, vanilla, and nuts. Beat well. Spread icing over cake in pan while hot. Cool thoroughly before cutting.
Mrs. Jack Edmiston (Candy)
Similar recipes submitted by:
Mrs. Frank Harwell (Edith),
Mrs. Toby Deese (Ruth Helen),
Mrs. James Luker (Judy), and
Mrs. Lawrence Hill (Gertrude)

CHOCOLATE POUND CAKE

"This is a real chocolate lover's delight."

2 cups sugar
1 cup butter
4 eggs
4½ ounces Hershey candy bars, melted
Water or milk
1 16-ounce can chocolate syrup
2½ cups all-purpose flour
¼ teaspoon salt
2 teaspoons vanilla
½ teaspoon soda
1 cup buttermilk

Cream sugar and butter. Add eggs, one at a time, beating well. Melt chocolate bars in small amount water or milk. Add bars and syrup to mixture. Add flour, salt, and vanilla and mix. Dissolve soda in buttermilk and add to mixture. Pour into greased and floured bundt or tube pan. Bake in 350 degree oven for 1 hour or until done. Cool. Remove from pan. Don't be surprised if cake falls.
Mrs. Stanley Thornton (Cathy)

Variation: Glaze may be added.

1½ cups confectioners' sugar
2 teaspoons cream cheese or butter, softened
½ teaspoon vanilla
2 to 3 teaspoons light cream
2 to 5 teaspoons nuts, chopped

Combine all ingredients except nuts. Beat at low speed until smooth. Spoon over cake. Sprinkle with nuts.
Mrs. Kenneth Barnes (Connie)

GRANNY'S POUND CAKE

"Old fashioned recipe – flavor improves with age."

1 pound butter
3 cups sugar
3 cups plain flour
10 eggs

Cream butter and sugar well. Add flour and eggs alternately, beating well after each addition. Pour into greased and floured large tube pan. Bake at 325 degrees for 1½ hours. Turn out of pan to cool.
Mrs. Ira Freeman (Enola)

GINGERBREAD

½ cup sugar
2 eggs
1 cup butter, melted
¼ teaspoon salt
1 teaspoon ground ginger
1 teaspoon allspice
1 teaspoon cinnamon
2 teaspoons baking powder
2½ cups all-purpose flour
1 cup cane syrup
1 teaspoon soda
1 cup hot water

Beat sugar and eggs; add butter. Sift dry ingredients together except soda. Combine egg mixture with dry ingredients. Add syrup. Dissolve soda in water; add to mixture. Mix well. Bake in large pan in 350 degree oven for 30 minutes. Top with sauce.

SAUCE:

½ cup sugar
Dash salt
3 tablespoons flour
1 cup boiling water
2 tablespoons butter
Juice ½ lemon
Rind ½ lemon, grated

In double boiler, combine sugar, salt, and flour; add water. Cook and stir until thick and clear. Remove from heat; add butter, lemon juice, and rind. Mix well. Pour over slices before serving.
Mr. George Robinson *Gold Hill, Alabama*

CARAMEL ICING

"A real treat, caramel icing – burnt sugar and butter."

1½ cups sugar
¼ teaspoon salt
¾ cup milk
½ cup sugar
½ stick butter
1 teaspoon vanilla

In saucepan, combine sugar, salt, and milk. Bring to boil over medium heat, stirring constantly. At same time, place sugar in heavy skillet and brown over low to medium heat while stirring constantly. Add to boiling mixture in saucepan. Stir constantly. Cook mixture to soft ball stage. Remove from heat; add butter and vanilla and beat until ready to spread. Will ice two layer cake. Icing will also freeze.
Mrs. Patrick Duke (Carolyn)

NEVER FAIL FUDGE FROSTING

2 cups sugar
¼ cup light corn syrup
½ cup milk
½ cup margarine
2 squares unsweetened chocolate
⅛ teaspoon salt
1 teaspoon vanilla

In saucepan, combine all ingredients except vanilla. Cook over low heat until margarine and chocolate are melted. Boil one minute or until candy thermometer reads 220 degrees. Remove from heat; add vanilla. Beat until thick enough to spread. Will ice two-layer cake.
Mrs. Julian Newman (Becky)

MARSHMALLOW FROSTING

2 egg whites
¾ cup sugar
⅓ cup light corn syrup
2 tablespoons water
¼ teaspoon cream of tartar
¼ teaspoon salt
60 miniature marshmallows
1 teaspoon vanilla

In double boiler, combine first six ingredients and cook while beating with mixer until stiff peaks form. Add marshmallows and continue to beat until melted. Remove from heat; add vanilla and beat to mix. Will ice two-layer cake.
Mrs. Guy Kaylor (Florence)

GERMAN CHOCOLATE ICING

1 cup evaporated milk
1 cup sugar
3 egg yolks
1 stick margarine
1 teaspoon vanilla
1 cup coconut, shredded
1 cup pecans, chopped

In saucepan, combine first five ingredients. Cook over low heat until thick, about 12 minutes, stirring constantly. Add coconut and pecans; mix well. Let cool at least 15 minutes before icing cake.
Mrs. Jay Thornton (Willene)

candies

AUNT EVA'S PRALINES

2 cups sugar
1 cup buttermilk
2 teaspoons soda
2 tablespoons light corn syrup
⅛ teaspoon salt
2 tablespoons butter
2 teaspoons vanilla
1½ cups pecans

In saucepan, combine first five ingredients. Cook over medium heat to soft ball stage. Remove from heat. Add butter and vanilla. Beat lightly until gloss is gone and mixture is creamy. Add pecans and drop on to wax paper.
Mrs. Patrick Duke (Carolyn)

PEANUT BUTTER BALLS

2 cups powdered sugar
6 tablespoons sugar
1½ cups crunchy peanut butter
½ cup margarine, melted
1 cup nuts, chopped
⅓ block paraffin wax
1 12-ounce package chocolate morsels

Combine sugars. Add peanut butter, margarine and nuts; mix well. Form into balls. In separate pans, melt morsels and wax and combine. With spoon, dip balls into chocolate mixture and place on to wax paper to cool. Makes 24 balls.
Mrs. Harvey Hall (Peggy)

BUTTERSCOTCH HAYSTACK CANDY

"A quick, easy but delicious treat."

2 6-ounce packages butterscotch morsels
1 6½-ounce can peanuts
1 5-ounce can chow mein noodles

Melt morsels in double boiler. Stir in peanuts and noodles. Spoon on to wax paper and cool. Makes 2-2½ dozen pieces.
Mrs. Lonnie Clevenger (Mary Burk)

MARY BALL FUDGE

4½ cups sugar
1 13-ounce can evaporated milk
1 16-ounce jar marshmallow cream
3 6-ounce packages semi-sweet chocolate morsels
2 cups pecans, chopped
2 sticks margarine

Combine sugar and milk in saucepan. Cook until boiling and continue to boil slowly, while stirring constantly. Boil for 13 minutes. Add remaining ingredients and mix well. Pour into greased 9 x 13 x 2-inch pan. Let stand 24 hours before cutting. Makes 5 pounds.
Mrs. Randall Stewart (Reba)

GLAZED PECANS

1 tablespoon water
1 egg white
2 cups pecan halves
½ cup sugar
1 teaspoon cinnamon
¼ teaspoon nutmeg
¼ teaspoon salt

Combine water and egg white and beat until frothy, *not stiff*. Add pecans and stir until sticky. Mix remaining ingredients and pour over nuts; stir until coated. Pour on to greased cookie sheets, spreading nuts apart so they do not touch. Bake in 325 degree oven for 15 minutes.
Mrs. Raymond Parks (Nada)

PEANUT BRITTLE

½ cup white Karo
½ cup cold water
1½ cups sugar
Pinch salt
2 cups raw peanuts
1½ teaspoons soda

Place first four ingredients into iron skillet or broiler. Cook until mixture is boiling well; add peanuts. Cook until mixture begins to turn brown or to cracking stage on candy thermometer. Remove from heat; add soda and stir until dissolved. Pour onto greased baking sheet and cool. When cold bend pan to break candy. Makes 35-45 pieces.
Mrs. Hubert Hubbard (Amie)
Similar recipe submitted by Mr. Bill McDonald *Anniston, Alabama*

DATE BALLS

2 sticks margarine
1 8-ounce package dates, chopped
1 cup sugar
1 cup nuts, chopped
2 cups Rice Krispies
1 teaspoon vanilla
Powdered sugar

Combine margarine, dates, and sugar in saucepan and cook until thick. Remove from heat. Add nuts, Rice Krispies, and vanilla and mix well. Cool. Make into balls and roll lightly in powdered sugar.
Mrs. Allen G. McMillan, Jr. (Jean)

ORANGE PECAN CLUSTERS

2 cups sugar
¾ cup fresh orange juice
1 tablespoon orange rind, grated
3 cups pecan halves

Cook sugar and juice in large boiler to soft ball stage. Remove from heat and add grated orange rind. Stir well. Add pecans and stir until mixture sugars. Spoon out on to wax paper.
Mrs. Brenda Jackson

CHOCOLATE COATED COCONUT BALLS

"These are wonderful to have during the Christmas Holidays."

1 stick margarine
1 14-ounce can condensed milk
2 boxes powdered sugar
Pinch salt
1 cup coconut
2 cups pecans, chopped
1 12-ounce package chocolate morsels
1 stick paraffin

In saucepan, melt margarine slowly and add milk. Stir in sugar and salt. Add coconut and pecans and mix well. Chill until mixture can be easily handled. Form into balls. Insert toothpick and chill until firm. Place morsels and wax into double boiler and melt over low heat. Remove from heat and dip balls into chocolate mixture. Place on wax paper and store in air tight container.
Mrs. Lonnie Clevenger (Mary Burk)
Similar recipe submitted by Mrs. Alden Limbaugh (Bobbie)

DIVINITY

"Never fail – very easy recipe."

2½ cups sugar
½ cup water
½ cup white syrup
2 egg whites, stiffly beaten
4 large marshmallows
1 teaspoon vanilla
1 cup nuts, chopped

In saucepan, combine sugar, water, and syrup. Boil mixture to soft ball stage or 230 degrees on candy thermometer. In large mixing bowl, beat egg whites until stiff. Pour one half of syrup mixture over egg whites, beating constantly at high speed on mixer. Return remaining syrup mixture to heat and continue to boil slowly until hard ball stage or 264 degrees. Pour over egg white mixture and continue to beat. Add marshmallows, vanilla, and nuts and beat until thick or mixture begins to lose gloss. Drop by teaspoon on to wax paper.
Mrs. George Hartsfield (Linda)

cookies

"HANG-YEN-BANG"

"Chinese Almond Cookies"

2½ cups all-purpose flour, sifted
¾ cup sugar
¼ teaspoon salt
1 teaspoon baking powder
¾ cup shortening
1 egg
2 tablespoons water
1 teaspoon almond extract
⅓ cup blanched almonds
1 egg yolk
1 tablespoon water

Sift together first four ingredients. Mix shortening and egg until creamy. Add water and extract; mix. Gradually add flour mixture, stirring until mixture draws away from sides of bowl. Knead to blend. Chill 1 hour. Form dough into 1-inch balls; using palm of hand, flatten to ¼ inch thickness. Place on greased baking sheet, ½ inch apart. Press almond into each. Beat egg yolk and water together and brush on cookies. Bake in 350 degree oven until golden. Makes 3 dozen.
Mrs. William Barton (Gladys)

OLD FASHIONED TEA COOKIES

½ cup margarine
1 cup sugar
1 egg
2 tablespoons buttermilk
¼ teaspoon soda
2 teaspoons baking powder
1 teaspoon vanilla
Flour

Cream margarine and sugar. Add egg, buttermilk, soda, baking powder, vanilla, and enough flour to make dough stiff. Pinch off small portions of dough and pat flat in hand or roll out and cut with biscuit cutter. Place on cookie sheets and bake at 300 degrees until lightly browned, about 10 minutes. Makes 18 large cookies.

Mrs. W. O. Woolley *Meridianville, Alabama*
Similar recipes submitted by:
Mrs. Walter Shivers (Lola)
Mrs. Alden Limbaugh (Bobbie)

HELLO DOLLIES

"A delicious goody at Christmas time."

1 8- to 9-inch graham cracker pie crust
½ cup chocolate morsels
½ cup butterscotch morsels
½ cup coconut, shredded
½ cup pecans, chopped
1 14-ounce can condensed milk

Pour morsels, coconut, and pecans into pie crust. Pour milk evenly over top. Bake in 350 degree oven for 30 minutes or until brown. Cool before serving.

Mrs. Randall Stewart (Reba)
Mrs. Curtis Lackey (Barbara)
Mrs. John Barksdale (Dorothy)

CARAMEL BROWNIES

1 stick margarine
2 cups brown sugar or 1 cup brown and 1 cup white
1 teaspoon vanilla
2 eggs
2 cups self-rising flour
1 cup nuts, chopped

In saucepan, melt margarine and add sugar, mixing well. Remove from heat and add vanilla. Add eggs and beat well. Add flour and mix. Add nuts. Pour into greased 13 x 9 x 2-inch pan. Bake in 350 degree oven for 20 minutes. Cool. Cut into squares. Makes 2 dozen.

Mrs. Denny Wood *Roanoke, Alabama*
Similar recipe submitted by Mrs. Merrell Sweat (Barbara)

COWBOY COOKIES

2 sticks margarine
1 cup brown sugar
1 cup granulated sugar
2 eggs, slightly beaten
½ teaspoon baking powder
1 teaspoon soda
½ teaspoon salt
2 cups all-purpose flour
1 teaspoon vanilla
2 cups quick oats
1 cup nuts, chopped
1 cup chocolate morsels

Cream margarine and sugars. Add eggs and mix. Add remaining ingredients and mix well. Form into balls and place on to greased baking sheets. Flatten balls. Bake in 350 degree oven for 15-20 minutes.
Mrs. Robert Wikle (Bernice)

FUDGE SQUARES

½ cup margarine
⅓ cup cocoa
2 eggs, beaten
1 cup sugar
½ cup flour
⅛ teaspoon salt
½ cup nuts, chopped
1 teaspoon vanilla

Combine margarine and cocoa in double boiler and melt over medium heat. Beat eggs. Combine sugar, flour, and salt and add to eggs. Add margarine mixture and blend well. Add nuts and vanilla and mix. Pour into greased and lightly floured 8-inch square pan. Bake in 325 degree oven for 30 minutes. Cool. Cut into squares.
Mrs. James Camp (Gayle)

CHOCOLATE COOKIES

1 12-ounce package chocolate morsels
1 14-ounce can condensed milk
¼ cup margarine
1 teaspoon vanilla
1 cup all-purpose flour
1 cup nuts, chopped (optional)

In saucepan, combine morsels, milk, and margarine and melt over medium heat. Add remaining ingredients and mix well. Drop by teaspoon on to greased baking sheets and bake at 300 degrees for 8-10 minutes. Cookies will be soft when done.
Mrs. George Hartsfield (Linda)

FRUITCAKE COOKIES

2½ sticks margarine
1½ cups sugar
3 cups flour
½ teaspoon allspice
½ teaspoon cloves
4 eggs
1 pound candied cherries, chopped (red or green)
1 pound candied pineapple, chopped (red or green)
4 ounces candied orange peel
2½ quarts shelled pecans, chopped
½ to ¾ cup whiskey (optional)
1 cup coconut (optional)

Cream margarine and sugar with flour, allspice, cloves and eggs. Add fruits, pecans, whiskey and coconut. Leave in the refrigerator overnight or until chilled. Drop onto an ungreased cookie sheet from a teaspoon. Cook approximately 10 minutes at 350 degrees. Makes five dozen cookies. For a fruitcake pour cookie batter into a greased and floured large tube pan and cook at 350 degrees until a toothpick comes out clean or the middle springs back when touched.
Mrs. Jerry N. Gurley (Cheryl)

SECRET KISS COOKIES

"Children love this cookie!"

1 cup margarine
½ cup sugar
1 teaspoon vanilla
2 cups all-purpose flour, sifted
1 cup walnuts, finely chopped
1 5¾-ounce package chocolate kisses
Confectioners' sugar

Cream margarine, sugar, and vanilla until light and fluffy. Add flour and nuts and blend on low speed. Chill dough. Remove foil from kisses. Using one tablespoon of dough, shape around a kiss, being sure to cover completely. Place on ungreased baking sheet. Bake in 350 degree oven for 12 minutes or until cookies are set but not brown. Cool slightly; remove to wire rack. While still warm, roll in confectioners' sugar. Cool. Store in tightly covered container. May roll again in sugar before serving, if desired.
Mrs. Robert Mullins (JoAnn)

CHERRY ROUNDS

½ cup margarine
¼ cup brown sugar
1 egg yolk
½ teaspoon vanilla
¼ teaspoon salt
1¼ cups all-purpose flour, sifted
1 egg white, slightly beaten
¾ cup pecans, finely chopped
⅓ cup cherry preserves

Cream together first five ingredients until light and fluffy. Stir in flour. Chill for 30 minutes. Shape into 1-inch balls. Dip in egg white; roll in nuts. Place on greased baking sheet, 2½ inches apart; press centers with thumb. Bake in 350 degree oven for 12-15 minutes. Cool slightly; remove from pan. Fill centers with ½ teaspoon preserves just before serving. Makes 3 dozen.
Mrs. Byron Boyett (Margaret)

ORANGE-COCONUT BALLS

1 6-ounce can frozen orange juice
1 16-ounce box vanilla wafers, crushed
1 stick margarine, melted
1 16-ounce box confectioners' sugar
½ to 1 cup nuts, chopped
1 7-ounce can coconut, shredded

Mix first five ingredients thoroughly. Form into small balls and roll in coconut. More flavorful when made at least one day before serving. Makes 100.
Mrs. George Ricker (Iva Nelle)

SPOON SUGAR COOKIES

"An old Southern recipe and very delicious!"

2 sticks margarine
2 cups sugar
2 eggs
1 teaspoon vanilla
2½ cups flour
2 teaspoons baking powder
Dash salt
1 cup nuts, chopped

Cream margarine and sugar. Add eggs and vanilla and blend. Add dry ingredients and mix well. Add nuts. Drop by spoon on to ungreased baking sheets and bake at 300 degrees for 20 minutes. Makes 8 dozen.
Mrs. David Beasley (Ellen)

GINGER SNAP COOKIES

¾ cup Crisco
¼ teaspoon salt
1 egg
1 cup sugar
4 tablespoons molasses
2 cups flour, sifted
1 teaspoon ground cinnamon
1 teaspoon ground ginger
2 teaspoons soda

Cream together first five ingredients until well blended. Sift dry ingredients and add one third at a time, beating after each addition. Form into one inch balls and roll in sugar. Place on greased cookie sheet, one inch apart. Bake at 350 degrees for 12 minutes. Remove from cookie sheet immediately. Cookies will flatten and crack while cooking. Makes 6 dozen.
Mrs. J. H. Johnson (Eleanor)

NUT BUTTER BALLS

"The butter makes the difference!"

1 cup butter
½ cup confectioners' sugar
2 teaspoons vanilla or 1 teaspoon almond extract
½ teaspoon salt
2 cups all-purpose flour
1 to 2 cups nuts, chopped
¼ cup confectioners' sugar

Cream butter and sugar. Add remaining ingredients except confectioners' sugar. Mix well. Chill dough until easy to handle. Shape into balls or crescents. Place on ungreased baking sheet and bake at 350 degrees for 8-12 minutes or until lightly browned. Sift confectioners' sugar over warm cookies. Repeat until sugar no longer sticks. Store in air tight container. Will keep a long time. Makes 3-4 dozen.
Mrs Byron Boyett (Margaret)

QUICK OATS COOKIES

4 tablespoons cocoa
2 cups sugar
½ cup butter
½ cup milk
Pinch salt
3 cups oats
1 cup pecans, chopped
½ cup peanut butter
1 teaspoon vanilla

In saucepan, combine first five ingredients and bring to boil. Boil one minute. Remove from heat and add remaining ingredients. Mix well. Drop by spoon on to wax paper.
Mrs. Randall Stewart (Reba)

GINGERBREAD MEN

"Great Christmas presents for the neighborhood children."

1 cup shortening
1 cup sugar
½ teaspoon salt
1 egg
1 cup molasses
2 tablespoons vinegar
5 cups flour, sifted
1 tablespoon ginger
1 teaspoon ground cloves
1½ teaspoons soda
1 teaspoon cinnamon
Raisins
Candied cherries
Decorator icing tube

Cream shortening, sugar, and salt thoroughly. Stir in egg, molasses, and vinegar. Beat well. Sift dry ingredients together and stir into molasses mixture. Chill about 3 hours. On lightly floured surface, roll to ⅛ inch thickness. Cut with gingerbread man cutter. Place on greased cookie sheets. Decorate by using raisins and cherries for eyes, nose, and mouth. Bake at 375 degrees for 6 minutes. Cool. Complete decorating with decorator tube. Makes 4 dozen.
Mrs. James W. Heacock, Jr. (Harriet)

FUDGY ICED BROWNIES

1 stick margarine
1 cup sugar
4 eggs
1 cup flour
1 16-ounce can chocolate syrup
1 cup pecans, chopped

Cream margarine until fluffy. Gradually add sugar and beat. Add eggs, one at a time, beating after each addition. Stir in flour and beat until smooth. Add syrup and nuts and mix. Pour into greased 9 x 13 x 2-inch pan and bake at 350 degrees for 25 minutes. DO NOT OVERBAKE.

ICING:

1 stick margarine
1½ cups sugar
⅓ cup evaporated milk
½ cup chocolate morsels
1 cup pecans, chopped

In saucepan, combine margarine, sugar, and milk and cook over low heat to boiling, stirring constantly. Let boil for one minute without stirring. Remove from heat and add morsels. Stir until melted. Add nuts and mix. Pour icing over brownies while both are hot. Cool. Cut into squares.
Mrs. James Barnett (Lynn)

RICE KRISPIE DATE BALLS

2 sticks margarine
¾ cup sugar
1 8-ounce package dates, chopped
1 teaspoon vanilla
2 cups Rice Krispies
1 cup pecans, chopped
Confectioners' sugar

In saucepan, combine margarine, sugar, and dates and bring to boil, stirring constantly. Boil until melted. Remove from heat and add vanilla; blend well. Add Rice Krispies and nuts and mix. Cool. Form into balls and roll in confectioners' sugar.
Mrs. Alden Limbaugh (Bobbie)

desserts

EMPANADAS

"Mexican Apple Turnovers"

2 cups flour
2 teaspoons baking powder
1 teaspoon salt
2 tablespoons shortening
Milk
1 21-ounce can apple pie filling
Confectioners' sugar

Sift dry ingredients together. Cut in shortening until well mixed. Add enough milk to form dough. Let stand 10 minutes. Roll out thin and cut into 4-inch circles. Place one heaping teaspoon of fruit on circle. Fold dough in half and pinch edges. Fry in hot deep fat until golden brown. Sprinkle with confectioners' sugar. Serve alone or with ice cream.
Mrs. Alton James *Mobile, Alabama*

SURPRISE DESSERT

"This is delicious to be so easy."

1 21-ounce can pie filling, such as blueberry, apple, etc.
1 box butter pecan cake mix, such as Snackin' Cake, etc. (one-layer size box)
1 stick margarine, sliced

Spread pie filling into small baking dish. Sprinkle cake mix over filling; dot with margarine. Bake in 350 degree oven for 30 minutes. Serve with vanilla ice cream. Serves 6.

Mrs. Jesse Foshee (Helen)

SCOTCH SHORTBREAD

¼ pound butter
⅓ cup sugar
⅛ teaspoon salt
2 tablespoons rice flour — add plain flour to make 1¼ cups

Cream butter, sugar, and salt. Gradually add flour mixture and mix thoroughly. Place mixture in round 8-inch pan and pat flat. Prick with fork. Bake in 350 degree oven for 30 minutes. Cut while warm. Freezes well and will keep for weeks in air tight tin.

Mrs. James Hood, Jr. (Eloise)

MACAROON PUDDING

2 cups milk, scalded
3 eggs, separated
1 cup sugar
1 envelope unflavored gelatin
½ cup cold water
1 teaspoon vanilla
1 dozen macaroons

Scald milk in double boiler over medium heat. Combine egg yolks and sugar and beat. Add to milk and cook until mixture coats a wooden spoon, about 20 minutes. Stir frequently. Dissolve gelatin in water and add to mixture. Cook 2 minutes. Remove from heat. Beat egg whites until stiff. Pour mixture over egg whites; add vanilla and stir slightly. Arrange macaroons in 2-quart casserole and pour pudding over macaroons. Refrigerate overnight. Serve with whipped cream or Cool Whip.

Mrs. Wallis Elliott (Dede)

BOCCONNE DOLCE

"This is an original Sardi's recipe – it's delicious!"

4 egg whites, stiffly beaten
Salt
¼ teaspoon cream of tartar
1 cup sugar

Beat egg whites, salt, and cream of tartar until stiff; gradually add sugar while beating. Line baking sheets with wax paper; trace 3 8-inch circles on paper, using cake pan. Spread egg white mixture over circles ¼ inch thick. Bake in 250 degree oven for 20-25 minutes or until gold but pliable. Peel from wax paper and cool on cake racks. Cover meringue layers with filling.

FILLING:

1 6-ounce package semi-sweet chocolate morsels
3 tablespoons water
3 cups heavy cream, whipped
⅓ cup sugar
3 pints fresh strawberries

In double boiler, combine morsels and water and melt. Whip cream until stiff, gradually adding sugar. Slice 2 pints strawberries. Place meringue layer on plate; spread thin layer chocolate over; cover with ¾ inch layer whipped cream and top with strawberries. Repeat layers. Frost top and sides with remaining whipped cream and decorate with whole strawberries. Refrigerate at least 2 hours before serving. Serves 8-12.
Mrs. William B. McGehee, III (Evelyn)

APPLE CRISP

"Peaches may be substituted for apples."

4 cups tart apples
1 cup sugar
½ cup butter
¾ cup flour
½ cup water
1 teaspoon cinnamon

Peel, core, and slice apples into a deep baking dish. Mix sugar, butter, and flour; sprinkle over sliced apples. Mix water and cinnamon and pour over apples. Bake uncovered at 375 degrees for 45 minutes.
Mrs. Crawford Nelson (Linda)

ANGEL FOOD CAKE ENID

2 egg yolks, beaten
2 cups sugar
¼ teaspoon salt
2 cups light cream
2 envelopes unflavored gelatin
½ cup cold water
2 egg whites, stiffly beaten
1½ cups heavy cream, whipped
1 10-inch unfrosted angel food cake, chunked
2 10-ounce packages frozen strawberries, thawed

In double boiler, combine egg yolks, sugar, salt, and cream and cook until mixture coats spoon. Dissolve gelatin in water; add to hot mixture. Remove from heat and cool. When mixture begins to set, fold in egg whites and whipped cream. Cover bottom of 9 x 13 x 2-inch pan with cake chunks; cover with custard. Repeat layers, ending with custard. Refrigerate until set, preferably overnight. Cut into squares. Top with strawberries and juice just before serving. Serves 14-16.
Mrs. Terry King (Peggy)

STRAWBERRY TRIFLE

1 package yellow cake mix
1 16-ounce package frozen strawberry halves, thawed
2 cups vanilla pudding
1 cup whipping cream, whipped
¼ cup sugar
¼ cup toasted almonds, slivered

Prepare cake mix according to directions on package. Bake in 9 x 13 x 2-inch pan. Cool. Cut cake crosswise in half; reserve one half for another dessert. Cut remaining half into eight pieces, slicing each piece horizontally. Arrange one half of pieces in 2-quart glass bowl; cut to fit. Pour one half strawberries and syrup over cake. Spread with one half pudding. Repeat layers. Cover and chill at least 4 hours. Whip cream and add sugar. Spread over trifle and sprinkle with almonds. Garnish with fresh strawberries. Serves 8-10.
Mrs. H. D. Kelly (Betty)

STRAWBERRY CREAM

"A sure-fire dessert and so easy to prepare."

1 envelope unflavored gelatin
¾ cup sugar
1 cup boiling water
1 cup heavy cream
1 cup sour cream
1½ teaspoons vanilla
1 pint strawberries, sliced, sweetened

Combine gelatin and sugar; add water and stir until dissolved, about 5 minutes. Add cream and mix. Chill until slightly thickened. Add sour cream and vanilla; beat until blended and bubbly. Pour into 1-quart mold. Chill until firm, about 2 hours. Unmold on to serving plate and spoon strawberries over cream. Serves 6.
Mrs. Walter Burt (Brenda)

BANANAS FOSTER

2 tablespoons brown sugar
1 tablespoon butter
1 ripe banana, sliced lengthwise
Dash cinnamon
½ ounce banana liqueur (optional)
1 ounce white rum
1 large scoop vanilla ice cream

Melt sugar and butter in flat chafing dish or skillet on stove. Add banana and sauté until tender. Sprinkle with cinnamon. Pour liqueur and rum over mixture and flame. Baste with warm liquid until flame burns out. Serve immediately over ice cream. Serves 1.
Mrs. Nelson G. Conover (Muffett)

OLD FASHIONED BOILED CUSTARD

"A special treat at Christmas time with fruitcake or jamcake."

4 eggs
1 cup sugar
Pinch salt
2 teaspoons vanilla
1 13-ounce can evaporated milk add homogenized milk to make 1 quart

In saucepan, combine first four ingredients. Gradually add milk while stirring constantly. Cook over low to medium heat 30 - 45 minutes or until mixture coats spoon. Refrigerate 12-24 hours before serving. Top with whipped cream.
Mrs. C. K. Compton Nashville, Tennessee

NORWEGIAN CHARLOTTE

1 pint whipping cream, whipped
1 tablespoon sugar
1 cup milk
1 teaspoon vanilla
2½ packages lady fingers, unfilled
⅔ 10-ounce jar red-raspberry jam

Whip cream, adding sugar. Coat large mixing bowl with cream. In a separate bowl, combine milk and vanilla and quickly dip lady finger halves into mixture. Place in bowl with cream; coat with jam and whipped cream. Repeat layers until all lady fingers are used. Chill. Spoon out to serve. Serves 12-14.
Mrs. Crook Nicholls (Sue)

GOURMET GRAPES

"Especially good after a heavy meal."

White grapes, seedless
Sour cream
Brown Sugar

Remove stems from grapes; rinse, drain, and chill. Fill individual serving bowls and add two tablespoons sour cream for each serving. Sprinkle well with sugar. May also serve ingredients separately on buffet.
Mrs. Thomas B. Richardson, Jr. (Elaine)

FRUIT DESSERT COCKTAIL

"A light dessert to serve after a game or turkey meal."

2 cups grapefruit sections
2 cups orange sections
½ cup sugar
Sauterne, chilled
8 maraschino cherries
Mint sprigs

Prepare fruit sections and combine. Sprinkle with sugar and chill. Divide into 8 sherbet glasses and cover with sauterne. Top with cherry and garnish with mint. Serve immediately. Serves 8.
Mrs. William D. Parker (Dorothy)

FROZEN EGGNOG CHARLOTTE

Apricot Roll:

1 cup sifted cake flour
1 teaspoon baking powder
¼ teaspoon salt
3 eggs
¾ cup sugar
⅓ cup water
1 teaspoon vanilla
Confectioners' sugar
¾ cup apricot preserves

Sift flour, baking powder and salt. Beat eggs until thick and creamy. Gradually add sugar, beating constantly until mixture is very thick. Blend in water and vanilla; add flour mixture, beating just until batter is smooth. Pour into a greased 15 x 11 x 1-inch pan lined with wax paper that has been greased. Bake at 375 degrees for 12 minutes or until center of cake springs back when lightly pressed. Invert cake on a towel dusted with confectioners' sugar; peel off wax paper. Starting at short end, roll up cake and towel together. Cool. When cool, unroll and spread with preserves. Reroll cake and place seam down until ready to use.

Charlotte:

⅓ cup sugar
1 envelope unflavored gelatin
2 teaspoons cornstarch
6 egg yolks
1 cup milk
3 teaspoons vanilla
¼ teaspoon ground nutmeg
4 egg whites
3 tablespoons sugar
1 cup heavy cream, whipped
7 or 8 canned apricots
½ pint whipped cream

Cut 10 to 12 slices from the apricot roll. Arrange slices against side and bottom of an 8-inch springform pan. Combine ⅓ cup sugar, gelatin and cornstarch in a saucepan; add egg yolks; beat until well-blended. Gradually stir in milk. Cook, stirring constantly, over medium heat, just until mixture is slightly thickened. Remove from heat; stir in vanilla and nutmeg. Chill in refrigerator until mixture mounds. While mixture chills, beat egg whites until foamy and double in volume. Add remaining sugar gradually until egg whites stand in soft peaks. Fold whipped cream and egg whites into the gelatin mixture. Pour into pan and smooth top. Cover with foil and freeze overnight or until firm. May be frozen up to 1 week. Garnish center with drained apricots, whipped cream and angelica. Serves 10.

Mrs. Jerry N. Gurley (Cheryl)

ROULAGE

5 egg yolks, beaten well
1 cup sugar
3 tablespoons cocoa
2 tablespoons flour
5 egg whites, stiffly beaten
1 tablespoon cocoa
1 tablespoon confectioners' sugar
1 cup whipping cream, whipped, unsweetened

In mixing bowl, beat egg yolks until pale. Gradually add sugar, cocoa, and flour while beating. Fold in egg whites. Grease and line with wax paper 9 x 13 x 2-inch pan. Pour in mixture and bake in 325 degree oven for 15-18 minutes. Turn out on to lightly dampened towel and cover with cocoa and confectioners' sugar. Roll like jelly roll while hot and let cool in towel. Unroll and cover with whipped cream; roll and chill to set cream. Slice and serve. Will keep in refrigerator for days. Serves 10.
Mrs. W. A. Davis, Jr. (Mona)
Variation: Icing may be added.

1 stick margarine
3 squares unsweetened chocolate
Pinch salt
6 large marshmallows
1 box confectioners' sugar
1 13-ounce can evaporated milk
1 teaspoon vanilla

In saucepan, combine first four ingredients and melt over very low heat. Remove from heat; add sugar and enough milk to make spreadable. Add vanilla. Drizzle over roulage or serve over slices.
Mrs. Barry McCrary (Marilyn)

GRACIE'S ICE CREAM

1 quart vanilla ice cream
3 tablespoons butter, melted
3 tablespoons brown sugar
½ cup pecans, chopped
½ cup cornflakes, crushed
½ cup brandy or bourbon (optional)

Soften ice cream. Mix remaining ingredients together and add to ice cream. Put into two freezer trays or any handy container. Cover with foil and freeze immediately before ice cream gets soupy. Serves 6.
Mrs. Fred Hahn (Martha)

VANILLA ICE CREAM

4 eggs, beaten
1 cup sugar
1 14-ounce can condensed milk
2 13-ounce cans evaporated milk
2 teaspoons vanilla
Milk to fill freezer

Beat eggs with mixer and gradually add sugar. Add canned milks and vanilla. Pour into freezer can and fill with milk to full line. Freeze. Remove dasher and pack until ready to serve.
Mrs. Walter Burt (Brenda)
Mrs. Wallis Elliott (Dede)
Variation: Add 2 10-ounce boxes frozen strawberries or 8 mashed bananas or 1 16-ounce can crushed pineapple, drained to change flavoring.
Mrs. Blake Harris (Mary Catherine)

HOME MADE ICE CREAM

"A very old recipe – handed down for generations."

2 quarts milk
6 eggs, beaten
2 cups sugar
¼ teaspoon salt
2 cups cream
2 teaspoons vanilla

Scald milk in double boiler. In bowl, beat eggs; add sugar and salt. Gradually add mixture to milk while stirring. Cook 3 minutes or until mixture coats spoon. Cool. Add cream and vanilla. Pour into freezer can and freeze. Remove dasher and pack until ready to serve. Makes one gallon.
Mrs. Hardy Conner (Becky)

LIME SHERBET

1 3-ounce package lime jello
1 cup hot water
Juice 2 lemons
Rind 2 lemons, grated
1¼ cups sugar
1 quart milk
1 cup cream
Dash salt

Dissolve jello in water. Add remaining ingredients and blend well. Pour into freezer trays. Stir one or twice while freezing to prevent separation.
Miss Eleanor Morris *Alpine, Alabama*

PEACH COBBLER

"Canned, sliced peaches in juice may be substituted for fresh."

3 cups fresh peaches, sliced, sweetened
1 tablespoon lemon juice
1 cup flour, sifted
1 cup sugar
½ teaspoon salt
1 egg, beaten
6 tablespoons margarine, melted

Place peaches into long baking dish. Sprinkle with lemon juice. Sift dry ingredients together and combine with egg, mixing until crumbly. Sprinkle over peaches. Cover with margarine and bake in 375 degree oven for 35 - 45 minutes or until crusty and brown. Serve warm with whipped topping or ice cream with a touch of cinnamon sprinkled on top.
Mrs. Alonzo Jones (Evelyn)
Similar recipe submitted by Mrs. Guy Kaylor (Florence)

FROZEN SOUFFLE WITH HOT STRAWBERRY SAUCE

1 quart vanilla ice cream
24 macaroons, crumbled
4 tablespoons Grand Marnier or orange juice
1 cup whipping cream, whipped
4 tablespoons powdered sugar
4 tablespoons toasted almonds, chopped

Soften ice cream. Stir in macaroons and Grand Marnier. Fold in whipped cream. Spoon into 8 cup molds or one 8 x 8 x 2-inch pan. Sprinkle with sugar and almonds. Cover and freeze until firm, 4-5 hours or overnight. Loosen edges of mold by wrapping with warm towel for 10 seconds. Turn out on to chilled plate and serve with sauce.

Sauce:

1 quart fresh strawberries or 2 10-ounce packages frozen
Sugar to taste
4 tablespoons Grand Marnier or orange juice

Clean and cut strawberries in half. In saucepan, combine strawberries and sugar. Simmer until soft. Add Grand Marnier and serve warm over souffle. Serves 8.
Mrs. William B. McGehee, Jr. (Mary Lib)

HOT FUDGE SAUCE

1 tablespoon margarine
1 square unsweetened chocolate
1/3 cup water, boiling
1 cup sugar
2 tablespoons Karo syrup
1/2 teaspoon vanilla
1/8 teaspoon salt

Melt margarine in saucepan over very low heat. Add chocolate and stir until melted. Slowly add water and bring to boil while stirring constantly. Add sugar and syrup and stir until dissolved. Simmer 5 minutes; add vanilla and salt. Can be made ahead and warmed over hot water before serving. Serves 6.
Mrs. Arthur F. Toole, Jr. (Barbara)

CHOCOLATE ANGEL FOOD DELIGHT

2 6-ounce packages chocolate morsels
4 egg yolks, beaten
Pinch salt
1 teaspoon vanilla
4 egg whites, stiffly beaten
2 tablespoons sugar
1 pint whipping cream, whipped
1 cup pecans, chopped
1 angel food cake, unfrosted, sliced

In double boiler, melt morsels over simmering water. Slowly add egg yolks, stirring well. Add salt and vanilla. Remove from heat. Beat egg whites, adding sugar and fold into chocolate mixture. Fold in whipped cream and pecans, reserving enough to top cake. Line 13 x 9 x 2-inch pan with cake slices; cover with chocolate mixture. Repeat layers and top with whipped cream. Sprinkle with pecans. Refrigerate for several hours before serving. Serves 12-16.
Mrs. Jack Wright (Joyce)

pies

PINK ADOBE FRENCH APPLE PIE

Pastry double crust pie
¾ pound tart apples, pared, sliced thinly
2 tablespoons lemon juice
¼ cup seedless raisins
¾ teaspoon ground cinnamon
¼ teaspoon ground nutmeg
¼ cup granulated sugar
½ cup brown sugar, firmly packed
2 tablespoons flour
2 tablespoons margarine
¼ cup pecans, chopped

Prepare pastry; line one 9-inch pie plate. Fill with apples. Sprinkle with lemon juice and raisins. Combine cinnamon, nutmeg, and granulated sugar; sprinkle over apples. In small bowl, blend brown sugar, flour, and margarine until crumbs form. Mix in pecans, and sprinkle over filling. Cover with pastry; crimp edges to seal; cut slits in top. Bake in 450 degree oven for 10 minutes; reduce heat to 350 degrees and bake for 40 minutes. Makes one 9-inch pie. Serve with sauce. May be frozen before baked.

SAUCE:

½ cup butter
1½ cups confectioners' sugar, sifted
1 tablespoon boiling water
1 teaspoon brandy or 2 teaspoons brandy extract

Beat butter and sugar; add water. Beat in brandy and serve with pie. Two teaspoons vanilla may be substituted for brandy, if desired. Serve pie warm so sauce will melt into pie. Makes 1 cup.
Mrs. Charles Nelson (Mary)

CRACKER PIE

3 egg whites, stiffly beaten
1 cup sugar
½ teaspoon baking powder
⅔ cup soda crackers, crushed
¾ cup pecans, chopped
1 cup whipping cream, whipped

Combine egg whites, sugar, and baking powder. Stir in crackers and pecans. Pour into well greased 8- to 9-inch pie pan. Bake in 350 degree oven for 30 minutes. Cool and top with freshly whipped cream. Let stand 3 hours before serving. Whip cream may be added prior to serving. Serves 6-8.
Mrs. George Montgomery (Andrea)

BLUEBERRY FLUFF

"Strawberry, peach, or cherry filling may be used."

2 cups self-rising flour
1 cup margarine, melted
1 cup pecans, chopped
1 8-ounce package cream cheese
3 cups confectioners' sugar
2 envelopes whipping topping
1 21-ounce can blueberry pie filling

In bowl, mix flour, margarine, and pecans. Pat into 9 x 13 x 2-inch pan and bake at 350 degrees for 15-20 minutes. Cool. Cream cheese and sugar together. Mix whipped topping according to package directions. Fold cream cheese mixture into topping and spread over crust. Top with pie filling. Can be made in advance and refrigerated.
Mrs. Jack Edmiston (Candy)

MACAROON PIE

24 salt-free crackers, crushed
24 dates, finely chopped
2 cups nuts, chopped
6 egg whites, stiffly beaten
2 cups sugar
2 tablespoons almond flavoring

Mix first three ingredients. Beat egg whites until stiff and fold in sugar and flavoring. Add cracker mixture. Place in large lightly greased baking dish. Bake in 325 degree oven for 30 minutes or until lightly browned. Cool. Cover with foil until serving time. Do not refrigerate. Cut into squares. Whipped cream and cherry may be added, if desired. Serves 12-14.
Mrs. Freeman Deitz (Miriam)

TOASTED COCONUT PIE

"For an easy to prepare dessert – yet so delicious!"

3 eggs, beaten
1½ cups sugar
1 stick margarine
4 teaspoons lemon juice
1 teaspoon vanilla
1 3½-ounce can coconut, shredded
1 8- to 9-inch pastry shell, unbaked

Mix all ingredients together in order as listed. Pour into pastry shell. Bake in 350 degree oven for 45 minutes. Serves 6-8.

Mrs. Harold Clark (Bobbye)
Similar recipes submitted by:
Mrs. Crawford Nelson (Linda),
Mrs. Ester DeAngelis Harrisburg, Pennsylvania

GIRDLE-BUSTER PIE

20 Oreo cookies, crushed
¼ cup margarine, melted
1 to 1½ quarts vanilla ice cream, softened
1 5⅓-ounce can evaporated milk
2 tablespoons margarine
½ cup sugar
2 squares unsweetened chocolate
½ teaspoon vanilla
1 cup whipping cream, whipped

Combine cookie crumbs and margarine. Place into 8- to 9-inch pie pan to make crust; freeze. Spoon in ice cream and return to freezer. In saucepan, combine next five ingredients and cook over low heat until sauce is dark chocolate color and smooth, stirring constantly. Let cool. Serve over pie and top with whipped cream. Sauce may be served hot. It is easier to slice pie before putting on sauce and whipped cream. Serves 6-8.

Mrs. James Barnett (Lynn)
Similar recipe submitted by Mrs. James W. Heacock, Sr. (Becky)

PINEAPPLE PIE

2 eggs, well beaten
1 cup sugar
1 8-ounce can crushed pineapple
4 tablespoons flour
1 stick margarine, melted
½ cup pecans, chopped (optional)
1 10-inch pastry shell, baked

Beat eggs until thick; add sugar. Drain pineapple, reserving juice. Combine juice, flour, margarine and mix well. Add to egg mixture. Stir in pineapple and pecans. Pour into pastry shell. Bake in 325 degree oven for 30 minutes. Two 8-inch pastry shells may be used instead of one 10-inch. Serves 6-8.

Mrs. David Beasley (Ellen)

MARSHMALLOW FRUIT PIE

"Any fresh, canned, or frozen fruit may be used."

½ pound marshmallows
½ cup milk
1 cup whipping cream, whipped
1 teaspoon vanilla
¼ teaspoon salt
1½ cups strawberries, fresh or frozen
1 8- to 9-inch pastry shell, baked

In double boiler, combine marshmallows and milk and melt. Cool thoroughly but do not allow to jell. Fold in whipped cream, vanilla, and salt. Pour one half mixture into pastry shell; cover with well drained fruit. Repeat layers. Chill at least 1 hour before serving. Remove from refrigerator 20 minutes before serving to take chill off pastry. Serves 6-8.
Mrs. Alec O. Thomson (Catherine)

APPLE PIE

Pastry for 2 crust pie
⅓ cup sugar
2 tablespoons flour
1 cup milk
3 egg yolks
1 tablespoon margarine
½ teaspoon vanilla
2 pounds tart cooking apples, peeled, sliced
1 tablespoon lemon juice
2 tablespoons margarine
2 tablespoons sugar
Dash nutmeg
¾ cup apricot preserves
1 egg yolk
1 tablespoon water

Prepare pastry and line one 9-inch pie plate. In small saucepan, combine sugar and flour, mixing well. Stir in milk. Bring to boil while stirring. Reduce heat and simmer until slightly thickened. In bowl, beat egg yolks slightly and add small amount hot mixture. Pour egg mixture into saucepan. Add margarine and vanilla. Cool. Prepare apples; sprinkle with lemon juice. In skillet, combine margarine, sugar, and nutmeg and melt. Add apples; sauté, stirring occasionally. Cook until almost tender, about 5 minutes. Remove from heat. Pour into pastry shell. Pour cooled filling over apples. In saucepan, melt preserves and spread evenly over apple mixture. Top with pastry. Beat egg yolk and water and brush on pastry. Bake in 425 degree oven 40 minutes or until golden.
Mrs. George Hartsfield (Linda)

BUTTERSCOTCH PIE

"A favorite recipe from Clairmont Springs Hotel."

1 pastry shell, baked
1¼ cups dark brown sugar, packed
½ cup flour
Pinch salt
1 tablespoon margarine
2¼ cups milk
3 egg yolks, beaten
1 teaspoon vanilla
3 egg whites, stiffly beaten
6 tablespoons sugar
¼ teaspoon cream of tarter

In double boiler, combine sugar, flour, salt, and margarine. Slowly add milk and cook until slightly thickened. Add egg yolks and vanilla and continue to cook until thick. Pour into prepared pie shell. Beat egg whites until stiff, adding sugar and cream of tartar. Spread over filling. Place in 450 degree oven for 5-10 minutes or until brown. Cool before serving.
Mrs. E. L. Barnes (Elizabeth)

CHESS PIE

3 eggs, beaten
1½ cups sugar
1 stick margarine, melted
1 tablespoon vinegar
1 teaspoon vanilla
1 tablespoon cornmeal
Pinch salt
1 9-inch pastry shell, unbaked

Mix all ingredients together except pastry shell. Beat well. Pour into pastry shell and bake in 350 degree oven for 40 minutes. Coconut may be sprinkled on top of pie, if desired. Serves 6-8.
Mrs. Dewitt Hanks (Christine)

LEMON CHESS PIE

3 eggs, beaten
2 cups sugar
2 tablespoons flour
1 stick margarine, melted
1 cup buttermilk
1½ tablespoons lemon extract
2 8- to 9-inch pastry shells, unbaked

Mix first six ingredients together. Blend well. Pour into prepared pastry shells. Bake in 350 degree oven for 35 - 45 minutes. Makes 2 pies. Serves 12-16.
Mrs. Charles Johnson (JoAnna)

4-LAYER CHOCOLATE PIE

1 stick margarine, melted
1 cup flour
½ cup pecans, chopped
1 8-ounce package cream cheese
1 cup confectioners' sugar
1 cup Cool Whip
2 4½-ounce packages chocolate instant pudding
3½ cups milk
1 teaspoon vanilla
Cool Whip

Combine margarine, flour, and pecans. Pour into 9 x 13 x 2-inch pan and bake in 350 degree oven for 15 minutes. Cool. Mix cream cheese, sugar, and Cool Whip until smooth. Spread over crust. Mix pudding, milk, and vanilla according to package directions. Spread over cream cheese mixture. Top with Cool Whip. One 13½-ounce container Cool Whip or 2 9-ounce containers may be used. Chill before serving.
Mrs. Harold Clark (Bobbye)
Mrs. John Barksdale (Dorothy)

LEMON LAYER PIE

"Preparation is time consuming but results are dependable."

1 9-inch pastry shell, baked
2 6-inch thin rounds pastry, baked
2 tablespoons unflavored gelatin
⅓ cup lemon juice, freshly squeezed
3 eggs, beaten
1¼ cups sugar
1½ tablespoons butter
Rind of 1 lemon, grated
1 cup whipping cream, whipped

Prepare pastry. In saucepan, soften gelatin in lemon juice. Add remaining ingredients except whipping cream and mix well. Cook over low heat until mixture thickens, stirring constantly. Remove from heat; cover and chill until mixture mounds slightly. Fold one half whipped cream into mixture. Spread one third filling into pastry shell; top with pastry round; spread one third filling on round and top with remaining round. Cover with filling. Top with whipped cream. Garnish with lemon peel. Chill thoroughly. Do not make too far in advance. Serves 6-8.
Mrs. Charles Nelson (Mary)

HERSHEY BAR PIE

5 ¾-ounce Hershey bars with almonds
19 large marshmallows
½ cup milk
1 13½-ounce container Cool Whip
1 8- to 9-inch graham cracker pie crust

In saucepan, combine first three ingredients and cook over low heat until melted. Cool. Fold in one half Cool Whip. Pour into prepared pie crust. Top with remaining Cool Whip. Chill for several hours before serving. Serves 6-8.
Mrs. Wayne Joiner (Gail)
Variation: 1 pint whipped cream may be used instead of Cool Whip.
Mrs. Guy Kaylor (Florence)

STRAWBERRY PIE

"Good for parties and club meetings."

2 cups sugar
2 cups water
6 teaspoons corn starch
1 3-ounce package strawberry Jello
2 pints strawberries
2 9- to 10-inch pastry shells, baked
1 cup whipped cream, whipped

Cook sugar, water and corn starch until thick and clear. Mix jello with a portion of this cooked mixture and stir until smooth. Add remainder of cooked mixture. Cool. Place one pint strawberries in each crust; pour glaze over strawberries. Place in freezer 20 minutes. Cover each pie with ½ cup whipped cream. Place a berry on each piece of pie when served.
Mrs. Tommy Barber (Betty)
Preston Wiggs

YUM YUM PIE

2 eggs, well beaten
1 stick margarine, melted
1 cup sugar
¼ teaspoon vinegar
½ cup coconut
½ cup pecans, chopped
½ cup white raisins
½ tablespoon vanilla
1 9-inch unbaked pie shell

Mix all ingredients well. Pour into an unbaked pie shell. Cook 30-40 minutes at 350 degrees.
Mrs. Nellie Ellis

PECAN PIE

6 eggs, beaten
1 cup sugar
1 teaspoon salt
6 tablespoons shortening
2 teaspoons vanilla
2 cups dark Karo syrup
2 cups pecans, whole or chopped
2 9-inch pastry shells, unbaked

Combine eggs and sugar and beat. Add salt, shortening, and vanilla, mixing well. Stir in Karo and pecans. Pour into two pastry shells. Bake in 325 degree oven for 45 minutes. Makes 2 pies. Serves 12-16.
Mrs. John Giles (Billie)
Similar recipes submitted by:
Mrs. Percy Williamson Anniston, Alabama,
Mrs. David Beasley (Ellen)

CHOCOLATE PIE

2 eggs
1 cup sugar
2 tablespoons cocoa
2 tablespoons corn starch
1½ cups milk
2 tablespoons margarine
1 teaspoon vanilla
1 8- to 9-inch pastry shell, baked
1 cup whipping cream, whipped
2 tablespoons sugar

Mix first four ingredients together in saucepan. Slowly add milk while stirring. Mix well. Cook over medium heat until thickened, stirring occasionally. Add margarine and vanilla and mix well. Pour into pastry shell. Cool. Whip cream, adding sugar. Place on top of pie before serving. Serves 6-8.
Mrs. Robert E. McBride (Margie)
Similar recipe submitted by Mrs. Pearino Gaither (Mary)

COMPANY PEACH PIE

"Make several for the freezer when peaches are in season."

1 stick margarine
1 cup sugar
2 tablespoons flour
3 egg yolks
2 cups peaches, sliced thinly
1 9-inch pastry shell, unbaked
3 egg whites, stiffly beaten
6 tablespoons sugar

Cream margarine, sugar, and flour. Add egg yolks and mix. Fold in peaches. Pour into pastry shell and bake in 375 degree oven for 45 minutes. Top of pie may be very dark. Beat egg whites until stiff, adding sugar. Spread on pie and return to oven and brown. Serves 6-8.
Mrs. James D. Luker, Jr. (Judy)
Mrs. Curtis Lackey (Barbara)

Talladega County Courthouse
by Billie Bliss

Special Menus

Elliot Home

by Wilmary Elliott

Afternoon Tea

LIME PUNCH* OR PINK CONFETTI PUNCH*
ICED COFFEE PUNCH*
CHEESE STRAWS*
SCOTCH SHORTBREAD*
CHERRY ROUNDS*
PARTY PUFFS* STUFFED WITH CHICKEN SALAD
PASTEL PETITS FOURS
GLAZED PECANS*

Warwick Home

by Wilmary Elliott

Sunday Night Supper at Sally's

CREAMED CHICKEN ON CORNMEAL MUFFINS*
APPLE SALAD*
BUNDLE BEANS*
LEMON CHESS PIE*

Home of Mr. and Mrs. Thomas E. Robbs

by Wilmary Elliott

'Tis the Season

EGGNOG*
WASSAIL PUNCH*
PARTY CHEESE BALL*
CHAFING DISH MEATBALLS*
FINGER DRUMSTICKS*
MARINATED MUSHROOMS AND CARROTS*
CRABMEAT A LA MORNAY*
SMOKED TURKEY WITH FREEZER BISCUITS*
CHOCOLATE PEANUT BUTTER BALLS*
ORANGE PECAN CLUSTERS*
DATE BALLS*
DIVINITY*

Home of Mr. and Mrs. Norman C. Wood

by Wilmary Elliott

Summer Luncheon

SUMMER SQUASH SOUP*
BROILED CRAB OPEN-FACED SANDWICHES*
ASPARAGUS MOUSSE*
CHEESE DELIGHTS*
STRAWBERRY CREAM*

ORANGEVALE
Home of Dr. and Mrs. Richard F. Bliss

by Wilmary Elliott

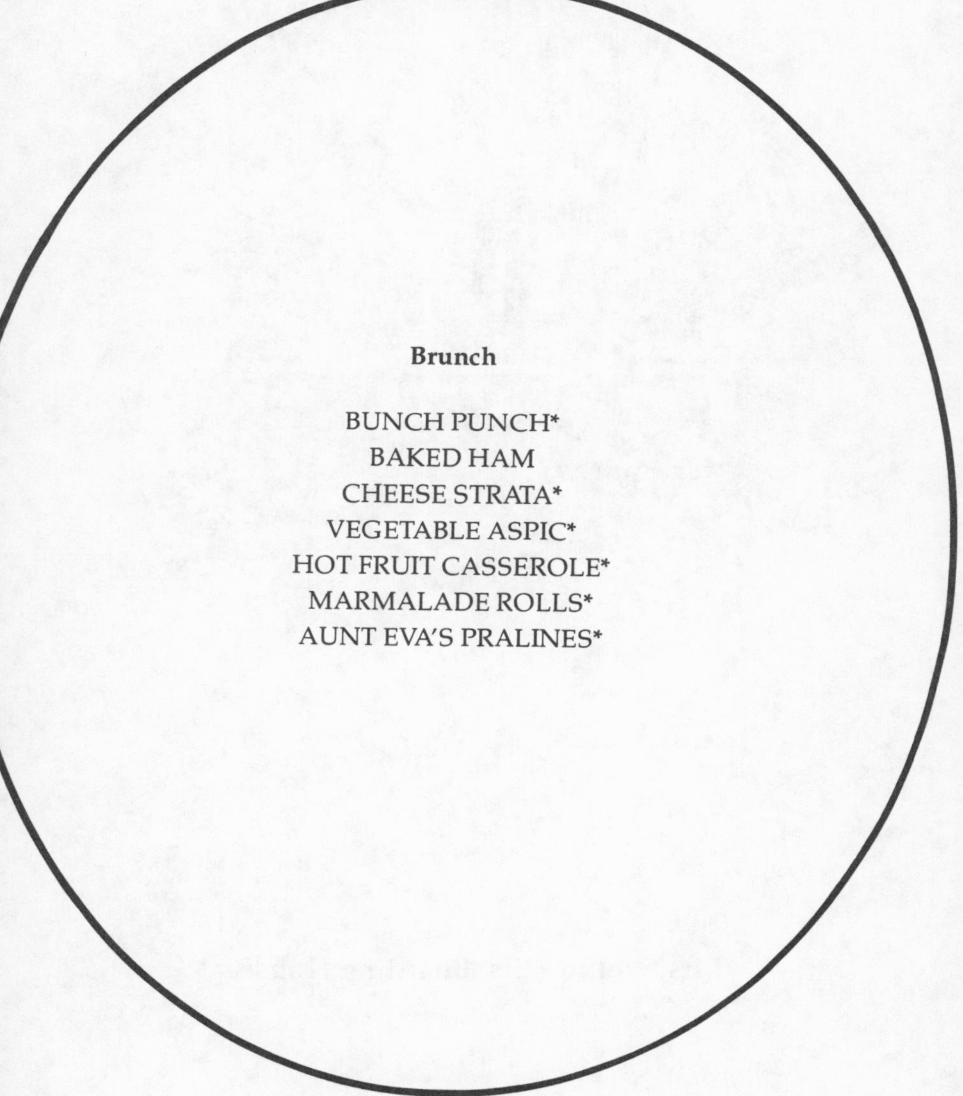

Brunch

BUNCH PUNCH*
BAKED HAM
CHEESE STRATA*
VEGETABLE ASPIC*
HOT FRUIT CASSEROLE*
MARMALADE ROLLS*
AUNT EVA'S PRALINES*

Mrs. Nellie Ellis' Boarding House

by Wilmary Elliott

Holiday Dinner

ROAST TURKEY
BAKED HAM WITH JEZEBEL SAUCE*
DRESSING AND GRAVY
MINCED OYSTERS*
SWEET POTATO SUPREME*
ASPARAGUS PEA CASSEROLE*
CRANBERRY FRUIT RELISH*
YUM YUM PIE* FESTIVE CAKE*

IDLEWILD
Home of Mr. and Mrs. William B. McGehee, Jr.

by Wilmary Elliott

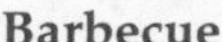

Barbecue

BRUNSWICK STEW* OR TENNESSEE HOT POT*
CHICKEN WITH TANGY BARBECUE SAUCE*
CRAB STUFFED POTATOES* OR GRANDMA'S BAKED BEANS*
TOMATO STUFFED WITH RITZ CRACKER SLAW*
DEVILED CORN*
FRENCH BREAD*
HOMEMADE ICE CREAM WITH BROWNIES

THORNHILL
Home of Mrs. H. Gordon Minnegerode

by Wilmary Elliott

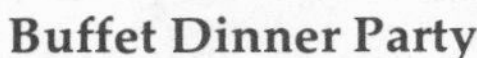

Buffet Dinner Party

SEAFOOD MOUSSE WITH ASSORTED CRACKERS*
BEEF BURGUNDY*
SAVORY LEMON-LIME RICE*
BROCCOLI WITH CHEESE ALMOND SAUCE*
JANIE RUTH'S FAVORITE SALAD*
EASY ICE BOX ROLLS*
STRAWBERRY TRIFLE*

EASY DINNER PARTY

CLAM DIP OR TRIO CHEESE BALL*
MOUSSAKA*
TWENTY FOUR HOUR SALAD*
HEAVENLY BREAD*
GOURMET GRAPES*

TERRACE LUNCHEON

CHICKEN CURRY FRUIT SALAD*
BROCCOLI SALAD*
ROLLS
MACAROON PIE*

MIDNIGHT BREAKFAST

SPICY EGG CASSEROLE*
SPINACH SALAD BOWL FOR 18*
BEER BREAD* OR BISCUITS
BLUEBERRY FLUFF*

TAILGATING AT THE TALLADEGA 500

RIBS WITH TANGY BARBECUE SAUCE* OR FRIED CHICKEN
ITALIAN POTATO SALAD*
DEVILED EGGS
CELERY STUFFED WITH PIMENTO CHEESE
DILLY BREAD*
BEER COFFEE
COWBOY COOKIES* CARAMEL BROWNIES*

FORMAL DINNER PARTY

ANCHOVY PUFFS*
EGG DROP SOUP*
SHRIMP VICTORIA WITH WILD RICE*
MUSHROOMS GRUYERE*
TOMATO ASPIC* AND/OR SPINACH LOAF*
AUNT JULE'S NEVER FAIL ROLLS*
BANANAS FOSTER*
CHABLIS

COFFEE

CREOLE DOUGHNUTS*
EMPANADAS (MEXICAN APPLE TURNOVERS)*
TOP HAT COFFEE CAKE*
QUICHE LORRAINE TARTS*
SAUSAGE PINWHEELS
ASSORTED SANDWICHES

BRIDGE LUNCHEON

CHICKEN-BROCCOLI CREPES*
FRESH FRUIT SALAD WITH POPPY SEED DRESSING*
CHEESE BISCUITS*
ROULAGE*

BRUNCH

BLOODY MARYS
CHICKEN LIVERS SUPREME*
CHEESE GRITS SOUFFLE*
CURRIED FRUIT* OR FRESH FRUIT SALAD*
WHOLE WHEAT ROLLS*

Alabama International Motor Speedway
by Karen Cleckler

Index

A

B

C

NOTES

NOTES

Junior Welfare League of Talladega
P. O. Box 331
Talladega, Alabama 35160

Please send me ____ copies of *When Dinnerbells Ring* @ $14.95 ea. ________
Please send me ____ copies of *Come & Get It* (sequel) @ $14.95 ea. ________
SUBTOTAL $________
(Alabama residents add appropriate sales tax) TAX $________
POSTAGE AND HANDLING ($2.50 EACH) $________
TOTAL $________

NAME ____

ADDRESS ____

CITY ____________________ STATE ____________ Zip ____________

Proceeds from the sale of When Dinnerbells Ring will be used for community projects sponsored by the Talladega Junior Welfare League.

Junior Welfare League of Talladega
P. O. Box 331
Talladega, Alabama 35160

Please send me ____ copies of *When Dinnerbells Ring* @ $14.95 ea. ________
Please send me ____ copies of *Come & Get It* (sequel) @ $14.95 ea. ________
SUBTOTAL $________
(Alabama residents add appropriate sales tax) TAX $________
POSTAGE AND HANDLING ($2.50 EACH) $________
TOTAL $________

NAME ____

ADDRESS ____

CITY ____________________ STATE ____________ Zip ____________

Proceeds from the sale of When Dinnerbells Ring will be used for community projects sponsored by the Talladega Junior Welfare League.

Junior Welfare League of Talladega
P. O. Box 331
Talladega, Alabama 35160

Please send me ____ copies of *When Dinnerbells Ring* @ $14.95 ea. ________
Please send me ____ copies of *Come & Get It* (sequel) @ $14.95 ea. ________
SUBTOTAL $________
(Alabama residents add appropriate sales tax) TAX $________
POSTAGE AND HANDLING ($2.50 EACH) $________
TOTAL $________

NAME ____

ADDRESS ____

CITY ____________________ STATE ____________ Zip ____________

Proceeds from the sale of When Dinnerbells Ring will be used for community projects sponsored by the Talladega Junior Welfare League.